Some today view journaling as a sentimental token of a bygone age. For others, it's a distraction from getting things done amid our frenetic pace of life. As one who has kept a journal since my teenage years, journaling has been an invaluable means of grace in my Christian walk and a practical discipline with many benefits. In *Imperfect Reflections*, Kirsten Birkett offers encouragement to keep a journal and write to 'know God better and to grow in godliness.' In these pages you'll find her at her favorite cafés throughout Sydney, Australia, reflecting on the craft of journaling and commending this practice best embodied in the Puritans. In a warm, breezy style, she writes as a fellow pilgrim in a world full of joys and sorrows. Whether you're a lifelong diarist or someone journaling for the first time, this book will serve as a helpful guide along the way.

Ivan Mesa
Editorial Director, The Gospel Coalition

Just this week I have been reading through and using a diary written from the early nineteenth century by an English Baptist poetess, and her words, detailing her theological and spiritual struggles, are poignant, searching, and helpful. It more than proves the argument that Kirsten Birkett makes so well in this compact study for Christians to be journaling. Birkett not only details why Christians should journal, but peppers her book with illustrations of the craft, helping the novice, as it were, to overcome any hesitations to put pen to paper. The book is ideal also for courses that deal with journaling as a spiritual discipline. I highly recommend it!

Michael A. G. Haykin
Professor of Church History & Biblical Spirituality,
The Southern Baptist Theological Seminary, Louisville, Kentucky

Journaling doesn't come naturally to us all, but it can be a transformative discipline. In this short, accessible book, Kirsten Birkett introduces us to the reflections of the Puritans and her own moving story, and in so doing helps us both taste the beauty of and engage in the practicalities of writing out words that are real, rich and re-orientating towards God. Ideal for those looking to take their first steps into writing. A great spur for those wanting to restart journaling after a break. An encouraging resource for anyone wanting to pursue Christlikeness with a Bible, pen and notepad in hand.

Helen Thorne
Director of Training and Resources at Biblical Counselling UK

I'm so pleased Kirsten Birkett wrote this compelling little book advocating for writing as a spiritual exercise, because I know how valuable writing down ideas is for thinking and learning. She has given us a deeply personal account of her own experience with journaling, and also many practical steps for using journaling as a strategy for living and growing as a Christian.

Rebecca Stark
Blogger at 'Rebecca Writes', 'Revive Our Hearts', and 'Out of the Ordinary'
Author of *The Good Portion – God: The Doctrine of God, for Every Woman*

Words are like magic. God's Word, and His words, are at the very heart of reality. And our words, not just spoken to loved ones and others, but thoughtfully formulated and carefully captured, in a journal, for our own souls, also can carry stunning power. Kirsten's discoveries about 'diary-keeping', as the Puritans called it, are not only compelling but time-tested. Our generation has neglected this ancient craft to our own impoverishment. It would not only do us much good, but give us great joy, to post far fewer words in public and journal far more in private. Rediscover the lost art.

David Mathis
Senior teacher and executive editor, DesiringGod.org
Pastor, Cities Church, St. Paul, Minnesota
Author, *Habits of Grace: Enjoying Jesus through the Spiritual Disciplines*

Imperfect Reflections

The Art of Christian Journaling

KIRSTEN BIRKETT

CHRISTIAN
FOCUS

Copyright © Kirsten Birkett 2022

hardback ISBN 978-1-5271-0846-2
ebook ISBN 978-1-5271-0922-3

10 9 8 7 6 5 4 3 2 1

Published in 2022
by
Christian Focus Publications, Ltd.
Geanies House, Fearn,
Ross-shire, IV20 1TW, Scotland.
www.christianfocus.com

Cover design by Laura Sayers and James Amour

Printed by Gutenberg

CONTENTS

To Amoni
for those chats over Australian coffee

Introduction:
How This All Got Started

From July 2018 to February 2019, I lived in Australia on a fully-funded writing fellowship. It was heaven; a time out of normal work life, to do what I most like, which is researching and writing. I arrived in the middle of a Sydney winter, which is, let's face it, like most people's summers. English summers, anyway. When it got to be Australian summer – it was Christmas in summer! Oh, how I had missed that – I had a week's holiday from the writing fellowship, which is like the buttercream icing on a luscious strawberry-vanilla cream cake.

Summer in Sydney is *hot*. I was living in a tutor's flat in what had once been the male single quarters of Moore Theological College, at that time empty for renovation. Moore College is in Newtown, an inner-city suburb which is normally hip, vibrant and, most of all, crowded. During the week from Christmas to New Year, however, it empties out almost completely. The non-stop traffic of the busy main road falls to almost nothing. Shops shut on the public holidays, there are no students at Moore College or the various colleges of Sydney University, libraries and offices close. It was during this time that I was able to think through something that had been on the back-burner for a few months.

Earlier, in my research on happiness, I happened to come across an academic paper written about the Puritan practice of diary-keeping. It argued (unusually for a secular publication) that this was not, actually, a sign of morbid introspection or evidence of Puritan self-flagellation. On the contrary, it was a spiritual practice that was kept up because it actually brought people considerable happiness and joy. It helped them turn depression or sadness or other negative emotions into positive ones; and the Puritans made a practice of doing this, because they saw rejoicing in God as such a good thing to do.

This struck a note with me, because keeping a journal does exactly the same thing for me. I write, mostly, because I feel bad about something, and by the end of writing I generally feel better. I have also used writing in my journal for specific spiritual ends – because I'm struggling to forgive someone; or I'm smarting from a well-deserved rebuke – and I want to examine what happened and help myself come to a godly response. I have never given much thought to this practice of mine. It has always just been something I do. If anything, I thought it showed a weakness on my part that I needed to overcome.

I have kept a journal since I was about eleven-years-old. Actually, I did so earlier in a way – I can remember writing down my thoughts from the time I learned to write, and keeping various small pink diaries with locks on them. But it was around Year 6 that I deliberately found myself a notebook – it was one of my schoolteacher father's hardcover, foolscap, lined books – and started writing down my thoughts, pretty much daily. Doing this continued to be my refuge through those awful teenage years. I remember that when I filled up the several hundred pages of that first notebook, I considered it my first book (not that I ever planned to publish!).

I kept up the practice in the years following, finding that writing down my thoughts not only clarified them, but that the practice was of immense emotional benefit. When I was afraid, upset, lonely or suffering any negative emotion, writing down what had happened and how I felt about it just made it better. Later on, I discovered that this is key to cognitive therapy and various other mechanisms to treat anxiety and other problems.

And here were the Puritans advocating exactly what I had been doing, only in an even more deliberate way. It was something they overtly recommended that Christians do, as a spiritual practice. I had, as I said, always been a little ashamed of my compulsive journaling. The only public advocation I had ever seen of journaling seemed to come from self-indulgent, privileged women with an interest in 'loving yourself'. I didn't want to be identified with this kind of self-focus, even though I secretly liked buying the pretty blank-paged journals that catered to this market. (I didn't know then that journaling has a very respectable following amongst North American Christians. Rather ignorant on my part.)

I know that journaling is a powerful counselling tool, and I have definitely benefited, myself, from the writing exercises involved in cognitive therapy. I knew that there were serious ways in which writing one's thoughts can be beneficial. I just had not associated this with my ordinary, everyday habits of keeping all sorts of journals and diaries.

Having been awakened to the Puritan practice, however, I now started to take my journaling more seriously – not just doing it, but thinking about what I was doing. Thinking about the way in which it contributes to my growth in the Lord, in working through the many problems of living a Christian life, of dealing with suffering and looking for God's wisdom. And in that glorious week, from Christmas to New Year 2018, I started writing a few chapters of what would become this book.

Other things have intervened since then; coming back to the UK, resuming my regular work, starting a new job, and then of course Covid and lockdown and my own suffering from the virus. The book took a while to get finished. Yet as I finish it off, I still remember those hot, hot days of summer 2018, the stifling flat in which I was living, the open-air cafes where I did most of the writing – so very different from my (rather cold) study, looking out onto a rainy garden in London, where I'm writing now. I enjoy writing, and it helps me. It helps me emotionally, but much more than that, it helps me know God better and to grow in godliness. I want it to help you, too.

1

Write

I want to encourage you about the fruitfulness of keeping a journal, not just as an excellent practice in itself, but for its spiritual benefits.

Indeed, diary-keeping has been popular for centuries. To the historian's delight, there have been many notable, as well as less-known, figures who were very diligent in keeping records of their lives. I have not made a detailed study of this by any means, but just off the top of my head I can think of figures from Queen Victoria, to Isambard Kingdom Brunel, Charles Darwin, and Gerald Durrell who kept journals which greatly improve our understanding of their lives and thoughts. It is a shame that it has fallen so far out of fashion. All the reasons that the Puritans gave for why it is a good thing to keep a regular journal (see the appendix), still hold. Let us revive the practice of journal keeping for anyone to do as a good thing in itself. In particular, what I am encouraging here is that it is an excellent practice for Christians, and a way of increasing godliness in ourselves.

Okay. Let me start my online journal

But wait. That's not actually what I am recommending. I want to encourage people, not just that we keep journals, but that we handwrite them. This might seem rather technophobic, not to mention a waste of time, in our age. After all, handwriting takes longer; and if I want busy people to keep journals, why not go for the easier route of the handy laptop or desktop computer? Isn't everything online these days?

True; and if in the end you decide that the only way you will realistically keep a journal is by typing it, then go ahead. But I would just like to give a plug for handwriting. Not only is it very pleasurable and relaxing, and gives the chance to add more artistic visual impact to what you are writing, I think there are actually real benefits to the practice of handwriting.

There is a lot of research on handwriting that emphasises its importance. For instance, there has been considerable investigation into children's learning, which shows that learning to write by hand significantly helps not just with language skills, but learning in general. For most children, handwriting is better in this regard than learning keyboard skills, even in our highly keyboard-oriented age. Chinese children suffer in their reading and comprehension if they do not learn to handwrite their characters. This might not be surprising, given the complexity of written Chinese language, but studies bear out the same conclusions for English-writing students.

When children do not learn to handwrite well, it can lead to serious consequences, not just for their further academic achievement, but also in such seemingly unrelated things as emotional well-being and the ability to function well in social situations. The student who can *handwrite* well is more likely to become the student who can *write* well – that is, the seeming purely mechanical skill of being able to put down thoughts, accurately and fluently, by hand, helps build the imaginative and creative power that enables the creation of written prose, whether fiction or non-fiction, even if the later writing is done on a keyboard. Children who learn to use a pen or pencil will become the students who do well in their essays.

Handwriting is actually quite a profound physical and mental process. It uses those parts of the brain that control visual and motor skills, but also calls on diverse cognitive and reasoning powers, and even uses parts of the brain that govern emotional functions. It exercises your powers of linguistics, attention, memory and physical learning.

Handwriting used to be an important part of the school curriculum in Western countries. Fine penmanship was considered a mark of education in itself, and was associated with character. Even gentlemen who could afford to have scribes do the writing for them, were expected to be able to write themselves. As teaching techniques developed, handwriting instruction moved from learning simply by copying models, to breaking down letters into individual strokes of the pen. Students would copy text painstakingly, doing drills of different letter shapes before stringing them together in words and sentences. Later, the idea developed that small children should be taught printing first. Cursive – joined up – writing was a mark of maturity; it involved endless practise of individual letters to be able to create a flowing hand.

Teaching methods changed, and learning started to be about children discovering the world for themselves, rather than memorising information the teacher told them. Handwriting drills didn't seem to suit this style of teaching. Moreover, as computers became smaller and even something that you could have at home on your own desk, keyboard skills started to take more prominence. Surely, teachers thought as they moved into the late twentieth century, it is more important for children to be able to type on a keyboard rather than to write by hand? With lessons starting to require homework on computer, and later iPads and other tablets becoming part of the teaching classroom, the ability to work a keyboard or touchscreen seemed to be the priority. It seemed far more relevant than the old-fashioned method of making marks on paper. After all, even if handwriting does require fine motor skills and cognitive development, so does typing – doesn't it?

However, handwriting is having a resurgence. Even with the prospect of much more home or distance learning, exams online or using computers in exam rooms, it seems there is still a place for knowing how to write well by hand. There is something about handwriting that seems to have a stronger connection to our personalities and ourselves than typing does. Research continues to show that handwriting is connected to the self in an intimate way that typing simply does not achieve.

Moreover, even as an adult, you will probably learn better if you use handwriting rather than a laptop to take notes. This is a much-debated question in university classrooms, but it does seem that even if you can take more complete notes on a laptop – because most students can type faster than they write – yet taking notes by hand helps you learn more, understand more deeply, and remember what you learned more successfully. Students who take notes by hand do better when they are tested on whatever it was they were taking notes about. This is true, even when the laptop students were allowed access to their own notes during the test. Part of this seems to be that, precisely because it takes longer to handwrite, students are forced to summarise as they go. This means that they process the information they are receiving, and so understand it better and remember it better.

I find that the very slowness of handwriting is part of what attracts me to it. When I put down my thoughts by hand, I process my emotions, and come to conclusions, in a far more profound way then when I do the same sort of writing by laptop. Computers are certainly more convenient, not least because if I compose a piece by hand I then have to transfer it to computer for publication, or to send to someone else. However, that piece will likely be better – better reasoned, more satisfying – if I have written it by hand first. Most of this book was written by hand, as I sat with my notebook in cafés, parks, restaurants or even at home by the window.

Handwriting creates a certain relationship between my thoughts and the words I use to express them. There is a kind of intimacy and privacy about writing by hand that is never quite the same on a keyboard. It allows the time for me to think through my thoughts, to see them forming before me. The stroke of the pen has a visceral quality to it, a sort of reality to it, that the feel of keys beneath my fingers, and the standardised typeface on the screen, can never match.

Certainly when it comes to journal writing there seems to be a distinct advantage to writing by hand. It is interesting that although the practice of journal or diary writing is centuries old, unlike other forms of writing it has not really adapted to the machine age. Most journal writers still prefer the handwritten method. When typewriters became dominant in workplaces and official writing, they were still never popular for private diaries. Perhaps the sheer noise and mechanical feel of the machine was part of the reason – but even the quieter computer keyboards still have some level of alienation about them. I want my thoughts, my words, to be mine; writing them by hand preserves that feeling far better.

Of course typing still has its place. You are reading my thoughts right now, and I trust they come through clearly even though you are reading a computer-generated typeface. However, imagine if you were reading my handwriting. It's fairly clear; although I'm quite capable of scrawling notes to myself, in general my handwriting is easy to read. Reading it, you would really know that is comes from *me*. A letter handwritten is so much more personal than a typed one; and that is not just a matter of convention or the effort involved in handwriting. My handwriting is like my signature, something that identifies *me*. Your own handwriting will be that to you, too.

The joy of being able to create your own page is part of the joy of handwriting. You may choose simply to write with a biro on lined pages. That is entirely fine. However you might enjoy using a different pen, the light touch of a fountain pen, the free feeling of a rollerball. You might like to use different colours depending upon your mood. Writing a page by hand means you can spontaneously glue in a leaf, or a feather, or a card or invitation that suddenly strikes you as something worth keeping. Scrapbookers know the pleasure of keeping photos in a physical album, adding commentary, small drawings, colourful margins. These things can all be done on your computer, but the sheer joy of manipulating the different materials by hand, feeling their texture and their physical reality, is simply not the same as formatting on your screen.

If you handwrite your journal, what is there is the immediate you. It may not look as pretty or as organised as a page printed from a word processor; on the other hand, it might be a beautiful record of you. You will not be able to delete mistakes, reword sentences or correct spelling as you can on a computer. But that is the point. Your handwritten journal is that much more closely connected to the real you at the time, the handwriting becoming rushed and scrappy as you write out your anger, the tear-blotted page as you write your grief, the sheer exuberance of the small smiley face or the exclamation marks you included as you wrote about your happiness. Your handwritten journal is a record of you. Don't put the extra filter of technology between you and the page. That's not what it's for.

(From an historical point of view, there is nothing like the handwritten draft! This is lost with computers. No longer will the historian have access to early mistakes, to the precious information that reveals how an author's ideas grew and developed. Musicians who compose music online rob the future of the chance to see a first draft of lyrics scribbled on a paper napkin or the back of a coaster, notes scribbled on manuscript paper with corrections and changes. We will lose the earthy impact of a diarist's handwriting, the first versions of novels. A manuscript, after all, is literally 'writing by hand' [*manu* means 'by hand', and *scriptus* means 'written']. All we have otherwise are digital traces in electronic memories.)

Don't ever underestimate the value of your handwriting. Thinking something to yourself can be powerful; saying it out loud even more so; but writing it down has a power to change your emotions and your brain itself. It is no accident that so many cognitive therapies involve writing down your fears, your challenges, and their resolution. The pen in your hand can change you, change your life. Take advantage of it.

2

Write Wisdom

Sydney, December 2018

I'm sitting in my favourite café in Newtown, a little hole-in-the-wall just down the road from Moore College, where (I will dare to say) they serve the best lattés in Sydney. And that's quite a claim. It's run by a group of young Asian men who are enthusiastic, great at customer service, and all make fantastic coffee. I come here often for takeaway when I'm working at Moore College, but the offices are all shut up and the library is closed this week, so here I am, working at one of the café tables. It's a small space, and the best table is the one by the wide-open window overlooking the street. As with all Sydney cafés these days, as soon as I sit down I'm given a (free) bottle of water and a glass – here it's served with lemon mint floating in the water bottle, which adds a delicious tang.

I feel so self-conscious writing in my journal, with a fountain pen no less, in a café. In a trendy Newtown café. It feels so pretentious. Like I'm trying to look all New York loft. Or is it San Francisco that has the lofts? I'm sure lots of places have lofts. Nonetheless, my little flat is hot and crowded, and this is a much nicer place to write. The breeze is not exactly cool, but at least it's a breeze. Probably brings the temperature down to the high twenties.

I have always thought of writing in my diary – what is now called 'journaling' – as my escape. It was absolutely necessary for getting me through my teenage years. It was my outlet when I thought I would otherwise burst, or dissolve, in my twenties. When I was diagnosed with depression aged 30, my journaling very easily morphed into the therapeutic exercises recommended by cognitive therapy. I carried my notebook everywhere, writing out my self-talk and challenges several times a day, for every event, sometimes both before and after. As the techniques became more automatic and the depression started to lift, I didn't need to do them quite so often. The daily, or almost daily 'diary' writing, however, continued; generally as a normal part of living, and sometimes a desperate necessity during emotional crises.

I realise now that it was always more than an outlet. It is part of (I think) what the Bible means when it talks of growing in wisdom.

It's somewhat similar to what happens when you download your life to someone close to you. Several times in my life I have had a close friend. Someone I would talk to almost every day, someone who was physically close by – one whose flat was in the same building as mine, later a friend who lived almost next door. Living so close, we would say hello and exchange a few ideas, every day. More often it was long conversations over a coffee in the morning, or after dinner, or any time. Yet life moves on, and each time I have had such a close friend, I have also lost the close contact with that friend – usually through her husband getting a job in another city.

It was the second time this happened, that I realised that one of the things I missed most about living so close to my friend was what I might call the 'doubling' of my experience. When I had a friend, I would get to experience everything twice – everything good, bad, funny, painful or just normal. I would experience it once as I lived it, and again that evening or the next day or whenever it was that I told my friend about it. What's more, the second time I would be able to reflect, analyse, laugh off embarrassment, share joy, hear my friend's sympathetic or amused comments – make it all so much deeper. Living the experience was one thing; understanding it, growing in wisdom from it, came the second time around. This was not just an incidental part of friendship. It was the way in which my own experience, and my friend's insight, became something that made me develop as a person. My growth in maturity was not just a matter of having experiences; it came from understanding what those experiences meant and how I could learn from them. In particular, how I could learn godliness from them.

Then suddenly my friend disappeared and my experience was singular again.

Writing my experience was what saved me. It's not the same as sharing with another person, but in some ways it can serve the same function. (Having a friend *and* writing – that's the best.)

We grow, not just by having experience, but by getting the meaning out of experience. It comes from recounting, reflecting and thinking. Why *did* I feel so bad when he said that? What was it about that comment that made me glow with joy? Why did that event feel strange? And what does it say about me that it did?

What does any part of my experience say about my view of God, too? It is the second time around, reflecting on my experience, that I get to see that what I do and say as I live isn't just about the situation, but about my character as I approach it. Did I feel uncomfortable because there was really something wrong, or was that just my pride because I wasn't as affirmed as I wanted to be? Am I feeling ashamed because I truly did something sinful, or am I just embarrassed because I looked a bit stupid? Maybe it was good to look a little stupid, because it meant I defied social norms to defend someone or go out of my way to care for someone. I can't always work out these things in the moment; sometimes my instincts are right, sometimes they are wrong. Thinking about it later – by which I mean writing about it, seeing what I think – means I can see more clearly, and more importantly, learn.

God teaches us wisdom in many ways. We learn directly from His Word (Prov. 2:6); this is the greatest and most profound privilege. We have communication directly from God, teaching us everything we need to know in life and godliness (2 Tim. 3:16-17). Yet our own personal reading of the Bible, while essential, is not the only way we learn. We also learn from others who teach us. The whole of the book of Proverbs is couched as a father teaching his son wisdom. We learn, too, as we seek to apply the Bible as we live our lives. Growing in wisdom is tied up in living, and practicing, and applying His Word to new situations as we make life decisions and deal with people day-to-day.

All of these things require thought; and sometimes we're all too slow to *think* about godliness. Yes, our godliness of character, our maturity, will probably improve just through the process of getting older and living life, as the Spirit works in us. But we do need to reflect on Scripture and what it is teaching us about each particular life situation, as part of our deliberate walk with the Spirit. I must continually ask myself, when I acted on instinct today, was that a good and godly instinct reflecting my knowledge of God's Word? Or was that my sinful nature telling me to put myself first?

Writing out what happened takes this a step further. It forces me to look at my behaviour, at my feelings at the time and now, and examine it all in the light of what I know from Scripture. It makes me slow down and take a longer view; put my instincts to the test, and reflect upon them. There is something more concrete and forceful about writing these things down, rather than simply thinking them in my head.

By this process of reflecting on life, on what has happened and my instincts in responding to it, I learn more about how to follow God. That's how I learn godliness. Otherwise, I'm all too quick to assume my instincts are right.

It's also true that the emotional reaction I have at the time will drastically colour my view, and it's not always right. If I come out of a situation feeling bad, I just won't have an objectively clear idea of what just happened. I need to deal with that emotional reaction first. Writing is the most powerful way I have found of doing so – this is what I have experienced during counselling, CBT, and about every technique for relaxation and stress relief that's out there (believe me, I've tried them all). Writing it out means I can understand my emotional reaction and deal with it. I can get over the strange embarrassment or distress, or whatever it is, and see if it was unnecessary, or stemming from pride, or actually justified. Writing it out lets me see whether I need to tell myself that I'm too sensitive, or whether I need to accept I was right, or whether I need to turn to God's grace for forgiveness. By writing, I can relax into joy when it's there, and not feel guilty or embarrassed about it. Writing it out means I can understand the feelings and feel better, or enjoy how good I already feel. It deals with emotion in a godly way, which I have learned I just probably won't do if I leave it to time, or even by thought alone without writing.

Writing works. It changes me, and I believe it can change you. I am advocating that you take it up, regularly, as part of your Christian life.

People have come in and out of this café, and no one appears to have given me a second glance. The waiter replaces my water bottle. I guess I'm not so pretentious, after all. Or even all that noticeable. That's a relief. What a lovely day.

3

Write Forgiveness

I'm sitting in my favourite little café again. Today, I've just come from the gym – it was a treadmill day today, and a long stretch afterwards, satisfying but not too hard, so I'm not exhausted, and I can enjoy my glow of virtue. The boys are busy cleaning, vacuuming, mopping, so I've been set back in a corner out of the way even though there's no one else here. I might move to a better seat nearer the door later. But for now this suits me fine. The music is vaguely soothing – the sort of thing you would expect to be played at very low volume during a facial, rather than medium loud in a coffee shop. Sure beats the music video channel they had blaring at the gym.

I want to write about forgiveness, and how to help yourself do it. I have three reasons for taking up this topic. First, it's something we will all have to do, sooner or later. We live in a fallen world and we are all sinners. You as well as me. You will do wrong to other people, and other people will do wrong to you.

We will have to go through life apologising for when we hurt others; and we will have to forgive others who hurt us. Which leads me to the second reason for writing about forgiveness: it is really, really hard to do. And so my third reason for writing about it is: even though forgiveness is so hard to do, it will help you to write about it. This is an area where your journal could be one of your key strategies in helping yourself do the right thing.

You may not have thought about this much. It may be that, in your life, you have not (yet) been sinned against in any kind of major way. Even so, there will inevitably have been small sins against you. We will all be sinned against, just as we will all sin. It's that kind of world. All the time there will be little sins, small matters of inconsiderateness, the driver who cuts in front of you, the customer who pushes ahead in the line, the man who offers obscenity on a bus. These things become easier to deal with as life goes on and maturity and wisdom grow – especially, I might add, if you are in the habit of writing about such experiences and so removing the annoyance or distress or fear they might have occasioned.

Then there are the medium-sized sins that are more painful when done to us. The boss who fails to keep a promise of promotion or reward. The friend who cheats you out of money. The sibling who takes unfair advantage of a parent. Wills, especially, can bring out shocking venality in what you might have thought was a happy family. I have been blessed with a family that does not fight over such things, but it can happen so easily. Greed is idolatry, and must be put to death, says Colossians 3:5: it is something we are all prone to.

Such sins are difficult to deal with. Injustice strikes us hard – the concept of being treated fairly is an innate sense within any person and we know when we have been treated unfairly.

It hurts. It hurts when perpetrated by a stranger; it hurts even more when injustice or unfair treatment comes from someone close. That hot, hard feeling of injustice – sometimes literally hot – it's no mistake that we speak of burning with injustice. It hurts. It's bad.

Then there are the terrible sins.

All sin is sin; all sins have the capacity to hurt. Some sins, however, are desperately awful, and hurt unbearably. They are the sins that can destroy lives, destroy trust, create scars that might never go away this side of glory. These sins can involve violence, sexual or otherwise; abuse, physical or emotional or psychological – we have all heard appalling stories and some of us know it firsthand. The unfaithfulness that takes away homes and livelihoods. Systematic fraud or inhuman treatment. Even in the safe West, with its legal systems and help networks, people are destroyed in private, in nice homes and tattered ones. In the countries from which refugees flee it can be public and endemic. This is a fallen, broken world and there is awful suffering.

How can we talk about forgiveness?

Some talk of forgiveness is far too glib. Some counselling can push forgiveness upon victims as if the crime never happened. Newspaper reports, it seems to me, can contribute by shallow reporting of, say, the forgiveness offered by Christian parents to their son's murderers, as if this was not a terribly costly offer out of deep love. Forgiveness is not easy. Ever.

Neither is forgiveness the considering of excuses. Excuses may be real. It may be true to say, he couldn't really help it – he was abused himself. He didn't mean it. We all say things we don't mean in anger. She's depressed; that's the depression speaking. It's been a really hot day, and tempers are fraying.

Any such excuse may be true, and might genuinely reduce culpability. Excuses, if genuine, can excuse people. They may well make forgiveness easier.

However, tough forgiveness kicks in when there is no excuse. It is what comes into play when you can't keep making excuses; when this person just deliberately, wickedly, hurt you. Unfairly and wrongly. That does not make a sin unforgiveable; on the contrary. That is when forgiveness is truly necessary. You have come into forgiveness territory, precisely because there are no more excuses. You can no longer excuse the sin. All you can do is forgive.

Forgiveness is not really optional. It is a command of Jesus repeated in all four gospels, and it is a necessary command, because it expresses the fundamental truth of reality. At the centre, the ground of this universe, is a God who forgives. A God whose property is always to have mercy, as the old Book of Common Prayer had it. Basic to our relationship with God is that He forgives us. What is more, He has forgiven us for more than the very worst crimes that any human can commit against another. Even the absolutely horrific ones.

That is almost unimaginable. We are so used to our own sin that, most of the time, it does not seem so bad. So we ignore God a bit. So what? So we're selfish and deliberately don't do what He wants and we're lazy about changing ourselves. So we're gossiping a bit, or cheating a bit at work, or putting our own ambitions for money first. So we follow our hearts for love even though we know we're doing things that are not really what God wants for relationships – well, those rules are kind of tough. A bit out of date. So we're not perfect. Well, who is?

God is; and we truly cannot imagine the appalling offence and pain it causes Him that His own creation, the living, thinking, loving people He created in love to love Him, would rebel against Him so casually. God is holy; He is pure, and we think our impurity nothing. He is light, and in Him is no darkness at all; and we think our cheerful embrace of darkness will not matter. It is intolerable offence to a holy being.

Yet He forgives; and His forgiveness also was more costly than we can imagine. Jesus suffered and died on a cross; the author of life, God who is eternal, experiencing death in the person of Jesus, who did not deserve it. He did not deserve it. There is no greater injustice than the death of Christ, He who loved life more than anyone, who created life and never tarnished it with His own sin.

Even so, we can be tempted to dismiss Christ's suffering. I have heard people, even faithful Christians, suggest that Jesus didn't really suffer all that much. Not really. It was over after three days, after all, wasn't it? Compare that to my suffering, I have heard people say. I have suffered for twenty years, thirty years, my entire life. I have an illness, a crippling, chronic pain, I grieve and it just doesn't stop. Don't I deserve some consideration for that? Jesus didn't do that much, people will say. Yes, sure, it was awful, but He died at 33; my suffering goes on and on. My suffering lasts a lifetime. My suffering has no such relief. Jesus can't understand the injustice I have suffered. He doesn't really know what suffering is.

It's a natural human response, precisely because we are sinful and we don't see things in perspective. Our own suffering will tend to colour our view of anyone else's. However, such a view totally misunderstands what Jesus went through for us. Even if the only suffering Christ experienced was during those three terrible days, such responses would be at best ignorant – if heartfelt – and at worst culpably callous. Nothing we can experience can compare with the immortal source of life itself experiencing mortal death, the sinless and holy God taking on the full weight of sin.

Yet consider this.

Though He was in the form of God, He did not count equality with God a thing to be grasped, but emptied Himself, by taking the form of a servant, being born in the likeness of men (Phil. 2:6-7).

The immortal God reduced Himself to the body of a helpless infant, and lived a human life in a sinful world. The immensely rich, became poor. He is the unlimited, all-powerful God. The most luxurious space-age super-yacht penthouse indulgence of a superior tycoon, would be to Him filthy squalor and an unbearable limitation in power. Think what it might be like for you to become a quadriplegic in the back alleys of some drug-ridden, Third World, lawless ghetto. That starts to suggest, possibly, just some small part of what it might be for eternal, omnipotent God to become human.

Yet He did it, so He could forgive.

Therefore the kingdom of heaven may be compared to a king who wished to settle accounts with his servants. When he began to settle, one was brought to him who owed him ten thousand talents. And since he could not pay, his master ordered him to be sold, with his wife and children and all that he had, and payment to be made. So the servant fell on his knees, imploring him, 'Have patience with me, and I will pay you everything.' And out of pity for him, the master of that servant released him and forgave him the debt. But when that same servant went out, he found one of his fellow servants who owed him a hundred denarii, and seizing him, he began to choke him, saying, 'Pay what you owe.' So his fellow servant fell down and pleaded with him, 'Have patience

with me, and I will pay you.' He refused and went and put him
in prison until he should pay the debt. When his fellow servants
saw what had taken place, they were greatly distressed, and
they went and reported to their master all that had taken place.
Then his master summoned him and said to him, 'You wicked
servant! I forgave you all that debt because you pleaded with me.
And should not you have had mercy on your fellow servant, as
I had mercy on you?' And in anger his master delivered him to
the jailers, until he should pay all his debt. So also my heavenly
Father will do to every one of you, if you do not forgive your
brother from your heart. (Matt. 18:23-35)

We must forgive, because God forgave us.

But forgiveness is hard, because we hurt. Forgiveness is costly. It means embracing unfairness. It is choosing, deliberately and openly, to accept injustice. It loves enemies who hurt us. That is forgiveness.

A few things:

Forgiveness means not taking revenge. We can do this because God is sovereign and just. 'Never avenge yourselves, but leave it to the wrath of God,' says Romans 12:19. 'For it is written, "Vengeance is mine, I will repay, says the Lord."' Forgiveness never means ignoring justice, for God is just and will ensure ultimate justice. However, it does mean leaving it to Him. Revenge is never right.

Forgiveness does not necessarily mean forgoing legal action. As citizens of a society we have a responsibility to assist with the keeping of order, and the legal system exists to see crime appropriately punished for the good of all. You can choose not to seek legal redress, but it is not wrong to do so. It is wrong to harbour fantasies of revenge in anger. Seeing a person appropriately punished for what is legally a crime is not. It is, after all, what government exists for (Rom. 13:4).

Being a forgiving person goes along with being an appropriately apologising and repentant person. You will sin against others. When you do, acknowledge sin and apologise. State what your sin was, say that it was wrong, and ask for forgiveness. Help others forgive you by showing that you truly know what you did, that it hurt and that it was wrong to do it. Don't say, 'I'm sorry you felt harmed'. Do say, 'I'm sorry I harmed you.'

Forgiveness might not bring reconciliation. If the other person is not repentant or refuses to acknowledge sin, you cannot heal the relationship as if sin has not happened. Some people will not repent. That is not your fault. Your responsibility is to forgive in your own heart, and decide to reject enmity.

Forgiveness does not mean being foolish or overly optimistic about a fallen world. A person might repent, genuinely, but might still be vulnerable to ongoing temptation. Forgiveness does not mean you have to put the repentant paedophile in charge of the Sunday School. It does not mean you put the repentant thief in charge of counting the collection. Be wise in your ongoing treatment of people.

But how do you forgive? What does forgiveness actually involve?

Forgiveness is a deliberate decision. It is the decision that you will no longer hold the person guilty. It means, also, deciding to take certain future actions yourself. It is deciding not to dwell on the sin, not to keep replaying it in your own mind so that your hurt feelings are continually given ammunition. It is deciding to make an effort to put it out of your mind. Forgiveness is also the decision not to bring up the offence again, in conversation or argument, against the person who sinned. It is the decision not to tell others about it, not to gossip about the person who sinned or make others view the sinner badly.

All this is hard, and if the sin is great, you will have to make these decisions more than once. Forgiveness is an ongoing process and takes time. Don't expect that you can change your heart and feelings with one decision. You will have to keep on making that decision, over and over, every time the bitter and hurt feelings come up again.

That is where writing comes in.

There will be hurt and anger and bitterness. Write it out. Get it on the page and out of your soul. Over and over.

Do it when you are awake at night mulling over the injustice. Don't mull; get up and write it down. Get it out of your soul and on the page.

Write, often and at length, what God has done. What He suffered. The injustice of His death. Just once won't heal us, but it will, for a short time, take the focus off your own hurt and onto His. Dwelling on God is always beneficial. It always helps, for anything. Write about His love. Write about how much He loves you. Look up Bible verses and copy them out. Even if it does not help straight away, it will be moving deep into your soul and starting the healing process. 'So shall my word be that goes out from my mouth,' says God. 'It shall not return to me empty, but it shall accomplish that which I purpose...' (Isa. 55:11). Trust God; His Word will change you, even if you can't feel it yet.

When you can, write a prayer for the one who hurt you. This might not be possible straight away. Even after a time, a one-sentence prayer of a few words might be all that is possible. Try; this is a crucial part of forgiving, that you are able to start wishing the person well. Try to work up to the stage when you can pray that God will forgive him or her. Then that God might bless him or her in some ongoing way. If the sin is great, this will be hard; never underestimate that. But if you persevere – and you must – it will also bring great blessing on you. For as well as never underestimating the hardness of forgiveness, also never underestimate the glorious freedom of being free of pain.

Expect it to take time. This might be something you do every day for weeks, months; it might be every week for years. It might be every now and then for the rest of your life.

Yet it is truly healing. The page can take your hurt. It can take your thoughts and absorb them. It can let them rest, take them away from that endless cycle that goes over and over in your mind, that keeps you awake at night and stops you from concentrating on your tasks during the day. Writing this all down can sooth your emotions and let them rest, even for a short time. Keep on doing it. It is worth it.

EXERCISE

Small sins: think of what you need to forgive; write out your hurt. Observe your reactions as you write and write about that. Think of God. Write a prayer.

Big sins: do the above, one step at a time, for the rest of your life. Or until the hurt is over. Whichever comes first.

4

Write Thankfulness

It's New Year's Eve. Public holiday! My favourite coffee shop is closed – good on them, I'm sure they deserve a break. So I'm across the road at the restaurant where I eat fairly frequently but I've never come here just for coffee. Or should I go to the coffee shop up the road? I don't know if it's worth the risk. What if I walked all that way and it was closed? It's *hot* today.

The tutor's flat I'm in is in one of the student accommodation buildings. The building is large, with a lovely cloistered walk at one end, then a long wing coming off the corner. I don't know how many students it would accommodate full – fifty? One hundred? It only had a handful of students when I moved in, as a lot of the building is being renovated, and now over the Christmas-New Year period, I think I'm the only resident there. My shared kitchen is down the end of a long corridor with no windows. Because of energy saving, the lights come on one by one as I walk along the corridor, then go off behind me. Slightly spooky, but also strangely liberating. I could run down the corridor singing and no one would know. Although I guess I could do that at any time; I like singing.

I am thankful about a great many things during this time in Australia. For the time itself, away from normal pressures. For the chance to see family – my niece and god-daughter has just had her first baby, and I've had the chance to get to know him in his first six months. I missed her wedding – London is a long way from Sydney, and especially tricky during term time.

I'm also very thankful to be here not depressed and not miserable. My CBT got me out of the black pit of despair and into functioning again, but it has been a long trek since then to get to stability and happiness. What an answer to prayer. I'm here, and here in this emotional state I pray I will stay – reacting normally and sympathetically to sad things, but without being thrown back into the abyss. Or even hovering over it.

This is a strange emotional land for me to inhabit. I have been catching up with old friends while here, and at one dinner recently I found myself thinking, 'This is the first time I've had a conversation with you and not been depressed'. It was very odd. It's also miraculous, which I say deliberately, at the same time as knowing what the intervening mechanism was. I can now take an interest in my friends' lives, and enjoy those lives, in a way I just couldn't before. I can hear of their joys and satisfactions and be happy for them, not reacting with envy or bitterness or withdrawal. Depression is not a sin in itself – it is an illness – but in that state I would so easily move to sin, letting my negative feelings take me into negative spirals of bitterness. It was all so easy to let misery and anger at what I did not have, destroy any thankfulness and joy in what I did have. It divided me from people as I both encouraged and bewailed my discontent.

It was awful; it has been a long battle to recover. Writing has been a large part of that recovery. It involved writing out my sadness, unloading it from my soul and then onto the page, turning to God. Writing out misery in my own psalms. Reading psalms that cried out my despair and seeing how the author turned to God, and writing my own desperate prayers that God would do the same for me. A lot of it I never want to read again – indeed, sometimes the act of throwing a journal away, or better still, burning it, has been glorious in itself. Watching that misery burn up.

I am very grateful for the change. Lots of different kinds of writing got me there. In more recent years, however, what accelerated it, what (I think) made for some of the most profound change of all, was writing thankfulness.

I first came across research on thankfulness when I was trying to find out what would make our students more resilient in their ministry lives. That was a fantastic, and fascinating, project to undertake. During my research, I read article after article about resilience as it is understood in psychological literature, read about training programmes to promote resilience in all sorts of stressful jobs, and all about counselling to promote resilience in those who have suffered trauma or have different kinds of mental illness. It made me understand a lot better what resilience actually is, and how we can help ourselves develop it. I also found out, somewhat to my surprise, that secular psychological research in a whole range of areas said that, in order to get resilience, we should do spiritual things. Do the sorts of things that the Bible tells us to do. One of the greatest of these – a 'supercharged' factor, as it was sometimes called – was thankfulness.

It was during this time, as I was discussing my research with people, and conducting interviews for my own research, I had a conversation with a student of mine about thankfulness. She told me of a book she had been reading. It turned out later that I had totally misheard her (the book she had read actually had quite a different title), but what I took away from the conversation was the idea of writing out 100 things to be thankful for.

Hmm, I thought, that's quite a challenge. It sounded worth doing, however, so I sat myself down, with a pen and paper, to try. I set myself the rule that I really did need to be thankful for the things I listed – no dutiful teeth-gritted writing down of things I knew I ought to be thankful for, even though I wasn't. I would write down one hundred things in my life, for which I was, genuinely, thankful.

It was surprisingly hard to do at first. After ten or so, I ran out. This is hopeless, I thought. God is so good! How could it be so hard to find things to be thankful for! My mind was blank, staring at the paper. But I was determined to finish. So I started small, with the room I was in. Little things struck me. My cat's purr. The particular shade of blue in my curtains. The fact that God creates colour.

It took a while, but I reached 100 things. The immediate effect on me was astonishing. To my surprise, and delight, I was incredibly joyful. Wow! A sure-fire way to find joy! My life was fixed! Unfortunately that joy was there only for a short, blessed time. It didn't last; soon I was back to my ordinary experience of that time, of being more or less constantly in a state of low-grade miserable nervousness. It certainly was no overnight cure.

Yet at the same time, it was the start of what came to be a huge and profound change in my state of mind. I'm talking about a long process of change; several years, in fact. Over time, I found that this practice of writing out 100 things, or a page, or two pages, or some other set, reasonably large amount, was deeply effective. When I couldn't sleep for worry, I would get up and write 100 things to be thankful for. When I was stewing in nerves, about to give a talk. When life and work were simply continuing to be a miserable grind. Not every night, but regularly, I would take up pages of my journal just writing a list of things in my life for which I was thankful. It changed me.

Anyone in the habit of reading psychology or counselling literature would probably not be surprised. Research on thankfulness is an exploding field, and it's proving astonishingly useful. Regularly practicing gratitude – mostly through writing things down – fixes people. It has positive results for depression, anxiety, eating disorders and addictions. People who are thankful are healthier, have better sleep and exercise more. I've read a fair few research papers by now, and I have yet to come across a negative result. Whatever the problem addressed, gratitude exercises as therapy has helped it.

So be thankful. It's good for you.

However, while I am all for mental health – and I am certainly grateful for my own recovery – this book is about godliness, not just healthiness. God created our physical bodies and minds, and it is not surprising if spiritual practices are good for us. But what I am interested in here is how to grow in godliness; in spiritual maturity, which means obedience to God, becoming increasingly like Christ in the ways revealed to us in Scripture. We don't want just to feel better – in fact, sometimes spiritual growth feels particularly bad, as we gain a deeper understanding of our own sin, for instance. Often it feels good, as we appreciate the depth of God's love. The goal, however, is to have our souls transformed. To become the sort of people citizens of the kingdom of heaven can be. To walk in step with the Spirit, being truly spiritual, more and more like Christ who is God.

I mentioned that my first list of thankfulness started with very small things, and mostly created things. That's fine; it is good and rich to notice the beauty of God's creation and be thankful for it. What was not on that first list, however, were things that might have struck a reader as surprising. Things you really would expect to find on a Christian's list. Salvation. Sacrifice for sin. The big things, the true doctrinal things which I knew I should be grateful for – and in my head and confession, I was, without lying – but they just didn't move me. My heart was left cold, except when singing a particularly stirring hymn, like 'And Can it be,'[1] perhaps. But not in normal life. There was some blockage between my head and my heart, or my brain and my emotions, and I couldn't seem to *feel* genuinely thankful for the things I knew I ought to be.

As for trials – well, there was no way I could list them as things to be thankful for. I know I was supposed to. I've read books by missionaries talking about how thankful they were for various hardships and disciplines God had inflicted, because of the spiritual growth and closeness to Him that had resulted. I couldn't do it. I wasn't thankful for trials and difficulties, for stress and pressure and rejection and loneliness. I wasn't thankful, and I didn't count any of it joy at all. I just wanted it not to be there.

That's a soul issue. That shows my immaturity in godliness. I was still saved, of course; still a Christian, still in the Spirit, still having every spiritual blessing and direct entry into the

---

1   Charles Wesley, 1738.

throne room of God. What Christ had done, living in perfect righteousness, always obeying God's law and letting me take the credit for that, dying on the cross for my sin so I don't have to suffer any penalty – that was still all true, all the time. I was just immature in not appreciating it.

That changed, and *writing* thankfulness was a large part of the change. It changed, as over and over again I reminded myself of God's goodness and love. As I opened my eyes more and more to how God works in this world and the wonderful things that result. As I saw that He *does* keep His promises; that hardship does test faith like a refiner's fire and makes it better. And that faith is so important, so valuable, so precious that strengthening it is the best gift I could have.

Now, my thankfulness lists include salvation; and even, occasionally, hard things about my life that I hate. I am, now, genuinely thankful for them – by which I mean that I *feel* thankful, and it's not a forced feeling. My heart has changed so that I do genuinely appreciate these things as good. I value them in my being and not just in my intellectual understanding. It means I believe, soul-deep, now, things I previously only knew in my head to be true. It means I have started to appreciate goodness in the world when previously I only saw what I didn't like. It also, paradoxically, means I see more clearly how much is bad in this world – and so feel deeply, gratefully, passionately moved by God's gracious entry into a morass of evil to save us from it.

Well, sometimes. I still have a way to go. I now look forward to it.

A friend recently commented to me that instead of bewailing moving into middle and old age, she wanted to see it as an opportunity to grow spiritually, to see deeper into God and so be more and more prepared for heaven. What a lovely vision. I will be truly thankful for the opportunity.

EXERCISE

Write out a list of things to be thankful for. Start with at least 50. Or go the whole hog with 100. It's okay for them to be small things. Read the list through and enjoy.

5

Write Prayer

It's New Year's Day, 2019. I just strolled across King Street Newtown – the main road, which runs down past Sydney University towards the city – without a car in sight either way. That is *astonishing*.

The restaurant I'm sitting in is crowded, which is not surprising seeing as there's nothing else open. I'm annoyed, even though I shouldn't be. After all, I'm all for businesses closing on public holidays: people need a rest, so I suppose I'm being hypocritical. But I'm not living in my own home, and my little tutor's flat doesn't have a kitchen, so I'm forced to eat out. This place is nice; a few tables inside, which I frequented during the cooler (can't really call them cold) winter months here. Most of the space, however, is outside, under a large awning that doesn't quite reach far enough. Today, there being such a crowd, there was only one table left; a little one, outside at the very edge of the awning, half in the sun. I have squashed myself over into the shaded half so as to avoid getting burned. The service will no doubt be very slow in such a crowd. No worries, I'm in no hurry.

I have with me on my Kindle a translation of some of the prayers of Anselm,[1] the medieval bishop and monastic. I've known him for a while and appreciate him as having some wonderful theology of God – he wrote about God's attributes, and also was the one who invented, or at least first published, the ontological argument. (If you don't know what that is, don't worry. Or google it. It doesn't really matter.) I had, however, never paid any particular attention to Anselm's prayers. They are deep and profound, and although I don't agree with his practice of praying to saints, his prayers to God and Christ are wonderful. I have not seen the Latin text, but the introduction tells me they are carefully crafted, rhyming and metrical, with clever word-play; works of art as well as works of theology. Moreover, he intended them to teach theology as well as express the Christian's heart. When he sent several prayers to the Countess Matilda of Tuscany, who had requested them, he instructed her not to read them too fast, but 'little by little, with attention and deep meditation'. He wanted her mind to be engaged and stirred.

I was a young Christian when I found out that a friend of mine was in the habit of writing her prayers. For her it made it more special; more formal, more thoughtful and weighty. I was somewhat taken aback. Surely God wants our prayers to be spontaneous, real, just as I would talk to anyone else? Isn't that the point of salvation, that we can approach God as a friend?

1   Benedicta Ward (trans.) *The Prayers and Meditations of St Anselm with the Proslogion* (London: Penguin Books, 1973).

From the heart, in normal language? Weren't formal prayers all churchy and somehow, well, wrong?

My reaction showed my lack of education as well as my naivety (and a poor understanding of theology, to boot). Also my lack of reflection. After all, I was already in the habit of writing thoughts and ideas – my method of thinking through ideas at all, was, pretty much, by writing them out. I also, in those pre-email days, wrote lots of letters (which meant I kept in touch with friends and family far more than I do now!), including letters to my pastor to ask questions. It meant I could be more exact about what I meant, more careful to say what was truly on my heart or exercising my mind. Why on earth would I not take the same, or more, care with God?

Christians have always written prayers. Scripture is full of them. The church fathers routinely included them. Augustine's entire *Confessions* is a work addressed to God. It is entirely appropriate for any work of theology – or history, or autobiography, or philosophy for that matter – to be addressed to God, and the *Confessions* is all of those. The introduction in my Kindle book of Anselm tells me, in fact, that it was a later innovation to separate works of theology from prayer. Actually, the earlier practice makes a lot of sense. It is surely only rational for our writing about theology to be addressed to God. Why on earth would we not? What is more, we surely want our prayers to be full of theology. It's the academic fashion now to see these as two entirely separate things; at best, God is addressed in the acknowledgements or perhaps the dedication. But why shouldn't works of theology be prayers?

The Puritans were famous for their published prayers.[2] They are very carefully crafted, with beautiful language and form. They are also full of theology, and I am often convicted by them in a way that I would not be if I just said my own, spontaneous prayers. Consider the honesty of this one:

> *O Lord,*
> *My every sense, member, faculty, affection, is a snare to me,*
> *I can scarce open my eyes but I envy those above me, or despise those below.*
> *I covet honour and riches of the mighty, and am proud and unmerciful to the rags of others;*
> *If I behold beauty it is a bait to lust, or see deformity, it stirs up loathing and disdain;*
> *How soon do slanders, vain jests, and wanton speeches creep into my heart!*
> *Am I comely? What fuel for pride!*
> *Am I deformed? What an occasion for repining!*
> *Am I gifted? I lust after applause!*
> *Am I unlearned? How I despise what I have not!*
> *Am I in authority? How prone to abuse my trust, make will my law, exclude others' enjoyments, serve my own interests and policy!*
> *Am I inferior? How much I grudge others' pre-eminence!*
> *Am I rich? How exalted I become!*
> *Thou knows that all these are snares by my corruptions, and that my greatest snare is myself.*
> *I bewail that my apprehensions are dull, my thoughts mean, my affections stupid, my life unbeseeming;*

---

2 Arthur Bennet (ed.), *The Valley of Vision: A Collection of Puritan Prayers and Devotions* (Edinburgh: The Banner of Truth Trust, 1975). Lately, I've been working through one such book, saying one, out loud, every morning.

Yet what canst thou expect of dust but levity, or corruption but defilement?
Keep me ever mindful of my natural state, but let me not forget my heavenly title, or the grace that can deal with every sin.[3]

What honesty! This is so much more real than just understanding the doctrine of sin. It challenges me because it captures my reactions so well ('what fuel for pride! What an occasion for repining! I lust after applause!'). This takes what might be just learned as 'theoretical' doctrine and turns it into real, heartfelt, soul-searching prayer.

I've mentioned before that I've found it very valuable to write my own psalms. It's valuable on so many levels. Just plain therapeutically, it's a chance to write out pain, get it out there, entirely privately express the real depths of hurt or misery or stress or whatever it may be. The written word makes it specific and concrete. It can be entirely honest; God can take it. Look at what some of the real psalmists expressed (see Ps. 6:2-7; 13:1-2; 31:11-13; 38:5-11).

A few years ago I was researching the concept of resilience. What creates resilience in people? Is there anything we can do to become more resilient people? I found, to my surprise, that a lot of the secular literature on resilience actually recommends things that are very spiritual. For instance, research shows that people who have a sense of purpose or meaning, and can see difficult life events in terms of a greater, spiritual reality, are those more likely to be resilient. It is good, then, to try to do just that – to find a way of framing events in terms of some greater purpose. It occurred to me, as I was writing and giving talks on resilience, that this is exactly what many psalms do. Psalms often

---

3   *The Valley of Vision*, p. 132.

start by presenting a problem or difficulty that the psalmist is going through, then remembering God and His plans, and then re-evaluating life in the light of God's presence. Many of David's psalms do that: they end on a positive note, because even the difficult things, enemies and sufferings and pain, grow smaller and easier to bear knowing that God is real and will bring salvation. Consider how the famous Psalm 23 does just this.

I started writing my own psalms, and recommending others to do so. Not at all putting my writing on a level with Scripture, but seeing this way of thinking about life as being very useful. When I write a psalm I put in writing whatever it is that is bothering me, reminding myself of God's promises and of the glory to come where there will be no suffering (for instance), and then concluding that my sufferings really aren't worth comparing with that. It always sets my thoughts on a more godly path, brings me more contentment, and makes me feel much better.

I really recommend this practice. Writing your own psalm is a great way to pray. It means that your prayers are not just bringing to God the real issues on your heart, but also that you are doing so according to *His* agenda. Writing a psalm also gives the format for working out some real theology. Just exactly what *is* God doing in this mess? we can ask ourselves. To answer, don't just try to invent an answer, or guess at some purpose: be informed by Scripture. Look at what the New Testament writers say – most of the letters were written to people experiencing suffering. Scripture doesn't necessarily tell us specific reasons for particular problems; but you can be reminded of the overall shape of God's plan, what He has already achieved and what He is achieving in building His church now. No matter what the problem facing you, consider who God is. Remind yourself of His greatness, His power, His purposes.

Consider, for instance Ephesians 1:9-10, which tells us of God's overall purpose for all things: 'which he set forth in Christ as a plan for the fullness of time, to unite all things in him, things in heaven and things on earth'. Or, say, Romans 8:38-39: 'neither death nor life, nor angels nor rulers, nor things present nor things to come, nor powers, nor height nor depth, nor anything else in all creation, will be able to separate us from the love of God in Christ Jesus our Lord'. Remind yourself that God knows what He is doing. Consider His love, His faithfulness; remind yourself how completely He has fulfilled His promises. He promised a land to Israel and gave it. He promised a Messiah who would deliver His people from sin, and He sent him. He promised a suffering servant who would have our iniquities laid on Him (Isa. 53:6); He promised a mighty Son of Man who would gloriously bring heaven itself (Dan. 7:13-14). And He did it – God kept His promises, no matter what it cost. God has promised that any suffering you go through will be worth it, will bring results more glorious than you can imagine. He will be with you and never leave you. He will let nothing separate you from Him, and He has never forgotten you.

Remind yourself of our wonderful future. Consider what Revelation 21:4 says it will be like: 'He will wipe away every tear from their eyes, and death shall be no more, neither shall there be mourning, nor crying, nor pain anymore, for the former things have passed away'. That's what we have to look forward to. Think about what that will be like, and write it down. This is all part of your prayer.

You could simply end there. That is prayer enough, and it is good for us to be reminded that prayer is not all about asking for what we want. Prayer is also remembering God, appreciating Him, and praising Him. It is thanking God for what He has done and for who He is. Prayer can be simply listing all the reasons why God is great. That's a great prayer to start the day with.

We usually have requests, however, and there is nothing wrong with that. In fact, Philippians 4:5-6 tells us that '...The Lord is at hand; do not be anxious about anything, but in everything by prayer and supplication with thanksgiving let your requests be made known to God'. It is precisely because the Lord is near, that He has brought himself near and enabled us to approach Him through Christ, that it is right to bring requests to Him. It is far better to do that, than to worry. Why waste time worrying about what might happen, when you have at hand the person who is actually in control of everything?

So, then present your requests. We're told to do it. It is the antidote to worry, and there is something about writing it down that impacts the heart more than saying it in our heads, or even aloud.

Maybe you have a gift for poetry, and your words can come out beautifully. Maybe you want to spend some time crafting your prayer and polishing the phrases. By all means do; prayer is special. Or maybe you don't want to. Maybe your words are raw, rough and hard. Maybe you would never write a poem in a thousand years. That's okay. You don't have to care about spelling or grammar; God doesn't. Write it anyway.

Your psalm, or any prayer, doesn't have to be just about suffering, of course. Pray when you're joyful. Write a prayer of thankfulness for your new baby, and keep it for your child to read in later years. Write a gratitude prayer for the new job, the promotion, the decision to leave work to accept much lower pay as a church worker. Write a psalm of celebration simply because

God is good and you love Him. Don't just let these moments of joy pass; write them down in prayer. You'll remember the moment better, and you can go back and savour it later. You will have taken time to express your thankfulness fully to God. It doesn't have to be a whole treatise. It can be your thank-you note to God. Consider it a kind of thank-offering.

Write a prayer of enquiry. In the middle of the essay you're working on for university or college, write a prayer to God about the question you're uncertain about. Why, God, did the Russian Revolution start? What is Keats saying in this poem? Did Henry VII really need to close those monasteries? God is always interested in what you are doing, and He knows all the answers – He made them! Not that He'll necessarily tell you; you still need to work on your essay, after all – but it's all part of your relationship with Him. How do I solve this equation? Why isn't my experiment working?

Write to God a prayer with your questions about your job. How do I talk to my manager about this problem? Why isn't this part of the project working? How do I approach that difficult colleague?

Especially write out theological questions to God. Why did Christ have to die? Are you really unchanging? Work out your theology in prayer, and when you've consulted the Bible and other theologians and thought about your answers, write thankfulness to God about it.

It all sits well with Bible meditation, of course, which is a later chapter. It can be exactly the same thing. There is no reason why your writing cannot be like Augustine writing his *Confessions*. (Read them if you haven't yet! Some parts get a bit dense, but most of it is fairly readable.) In that, Augustine was partly remembering and reflecting on his life, partly working out theological problems, partly writing down all sorts of musings about what is right and how to act: and it is all addressed to God as prayer.

PSALM 3

O LORD, how many are my foes!
Many are rising against me; many are saying of my soul, "There is no salvation for him in God."
But you, O LORD, are a shield about me, my glory, and the lifter of my head.
I cried aloud to the LORD, and he answered me from his holy hill.
I lay down and slept; I woke again, for the LORD sustained me.
I will not be afraid of many thousands of people who have set themselves against me all around.
Arise, O LORD!
Save me, O my God!
For you strike all my enemies on the cheek; you break the teeth of the wicked.
Salvation belongs to the LORD; your blessing be on your people!

PSALM 133

Behold, how good and pleasant it is
when brothers dwell in unity!
It is like the precious foil on the head,
running down on the beard,
on the beard of Aaron,
running down on the collar of his robes!
It is like the dew of Hermon,
which falls on the mountains of Zion!

For there the LORD has commanded the blessing,
life forevermore.

Write a psalm.

POSTSCRIPT

The sun is moving in, not out, so I've had to shift to another table: I've been here over an hour, and it's slightly less busy now, so more tables are free. I've ordered another coffee – decaf this time, or else I'll blow my limit. Artificial anxiety I do not need. The waitress brings me my third bottle of water. The breeze is warm, but soft; the background voices cheerful. 'Let's go to the beach', says the man to the woman with him at the next table; they get up and leave. I don't envy them – any local Sydney beach will be packed solid today, and the sun is hot and burny. I'll stay here in the shade of the coffee shop and enjoy my latte. Thank you, Lord.

6

Write Witness

It's the Sunday after New Year, 2019, and I'm at a different café this time: the Grumpy Baker in Bellevue Hill. Good coffee again, of course. I must take this opportunity to celebrate Sydney coffee. London, you don't know what you're missing. I don't need to go to any kind of specialist coffee shop here, just any old local café has coffee that sends my soul soaring. Ah, the joy of a fantastic coffee in the Sydney sunshine.

I'm eating a protein ball thingy – I never really know what to call them, so I just point at the jar. It is rich and delicious, and I can pretend it's healthy. I decided to sit outside, even though it's pretty hot – inside is only minimally cooler, as there's no air-conditioning and it's all open to the outside. I walked up from Bondi Junction with no hat, so I'm probably a bit sunburned; my UK skin has yet to get properly used to Australian sun again. I keep finding myself without a hat, even though I keep buying them. I'm terrible with losing things like that; they get themselves left on trains, in libraries, or who knows where. I've lost two really nice hats since being here in Sydney. Hats, umbrellas, even coats – they all go the way of such things eventually. To the Lost Land of Accessories. I would love to visit there.

An Indian myna bird is looking avariciously at my protein ball. Better eat it.

I've been attending church at St Andrew's Cathedral in Sydney since I've been here. Church at the Cathedral this morning was lovely. The Cathedral is in holiday mode, so no choir, just all congregational singing. All the hymns were Christmas carols – good to see; it is Christmas season until 5th January, after all. (My traditional Anglicanism is coming out.) The Dean of the cathedral, my friend Kanishka, preached a great sermon on Romans 8:1-7. He spoke of the glorious saving gospel which tells us that Jesus was sent to do what the law could not. Jesus took on human flesh to be a sacrifice for sin. He became man and He died for us, taking the death penalty that we all deserve for turning away from God. Christmas and Easter in one sentence. Jesus became human for us – that's the Incarnation, the Christmas story. God who is eternal and infinite and pure, took on human flesh, so that He could be a proper substitute for other humans. He became the second Adam, so that He could reverse the curse that the first Adam brought into the world, reverse the death penalty that has reigned in this fallen world since Adam, the representative of the whole human race, who rejected God and His Word. Jesus became human so He could die, because immortal God in His divine nature cannot die.

Jesus died for us – that's the atonement, the Easter story. He died the death that we all deserve – not just the physical death, the spiritual death which means separation from God who is life itself. Jesus had to have a human nature in order to be able to die, to experience death. He was the sacrifice for our sin. It was a perfect sacrifice, sufficient to pay for all sin, every sin we will commit, past, present and future. He didn't deserve to die, because He never sinned. But He died for our sin. He took God's anger at our sin on himself, so that we never have to experience it for ourselves. It was terrible for Him. Blessedly wonderful for us.

And then Jesus rose again – the resurrection. In Him, we can now live new lives, free from the bondage to sin, free from its penalty. The righteousness, the sinlessness that was Jesus' life, we are now allowed to claim for ourselves. We don't deserve that credit, but God so generously gives it to us. It is what will enable us to get into heaven – Jesus' righteousness, not our own. It means that now, we can live spiritual lives. We can live in relationship with God, not afraid, not under the burden of possible punishment, because Jesus has done it all for us. We can start a joyful eternal life, now.

It's the truth I have known for over thirty years now, and it's still fresh, good news every time I hear it. God truly exists, and He truly loves us, and proved it by coming into our broken world to heal it. He makes spiritual living possible.

It's wonderful and I wish everyone knew it. I wish all my friends and family knew it. I can't make them embrace it, but I wish I could tell them just how unimaginably lovely it is what God has done. I wish I could share with them what joy they could have, the eternal life they could have. I wish I could tell them, explain to them this truth, so they could understand it and take it on in their own lives.

Trouble is, I'm not very good at doing that.

I'm not very good at talking to people. I grew up as what people call 'painfully shy' – people say that without really reflecting on, or perhaps even realising, just how painful it is. Just get out there and talk to people, I was told. Go to that party. You'll enjoy it once you get there. If you don't get out and make friends, the only person who will suffer is you.

Well, no. I suffered when I did make the effort to talk to people. I went to the parties, the youth group, the school socials, usually pushed to go, and I didn't enjoy it once I got there. I'm the only person I know who, as a teenager, got into trouble for staying home doing homework instead of going out drinking with friends. (It was boring, so I came home.)

When I reached university I suffered the compulsory socialising for a while but eventually decided to just stop. In fact, to stop talking to people altogether. Seriously. I had a flatmate – couldn't afford to live alone – but he worked two jobs so was conveniently not there most of the time. There was no phone connected (again, too expensive) and this was before mobiles, so no easy way for anyone to contact me or for me to talk to them. If I really needed to contact someone (well, my parents, who quite rightly expected me to call regularly) I would walk down the road to a public phone box. Most of the time, however, I could quite successfully avoid anyone. If I saw someone I knew, I would cross the road. Genuinely; I would actually do that. I sat by myself in lectures – universities are a place, I discovered, where it is very easy to remain totally alone and anonymous. I was disconnected, and avoidant.

That's literally true, actually; I was eventually diagnosed with what is known as avoidant personality disorder, a condition where people avoid social situations that are difficult, whose personalities are such that they always tend to avoid other people. I was also diagnosed with social phobia, which is a particular form of social shyness in which (amongst other things) new situations don't get better with time. So there. I knew I wouldn't enjoy it once I got there.

These anxiety conditions also cause acute depression. I was treated very successfully with Cognitive Behavioural Therapy, then relatively new, but in my case extremely helpful. But that diagnosis, and the treatment, did not come until I was 30. In the meantime, I had my twenties to get through – and that was difficult, because in my second year of university I became a Christian. Wonderful, yes; glorious to discover the truth about the universe and to know God, and, of course, to receive complete salvation from sin. But now I had a reason to talk to people. People matter, I discovered; it's not okay to ignore them. I had to get over my fear. Even more than that, I found out that God wants His saving message, this miraculous truth about Himself and what He has done for us, to spread through the bizarrely humble method of just ordinary people talking to other people. God speaks in words. His gospel is good news. It's a message, not just an experience. We must always be ready to give answers about the hope we have; He sends apostles, prophets, preachers, teachers, and ministers of the word to tell and teach the message. It means talking to people.

The trouble is, knowing that God wanted me to talk to people didn't make me any good at it. It certainly didn't make it any easier.

I tried – I tried very hard. I watched people and listened to how they spoke. I would stand in small conversational groups after church, not really knowing what to say, but observing how other people did it. I learned that there are conversations where people take turns telling stories. There are others when they take turns asking questions and answering. I learned that the best way to talk to someone is to ask questions a lot, and to listen a lot.

As I mentioned, my therapy for my social anxiety and the depression it had spawned, was very successful. I was no longer totally floored by social situations. I also learned more skills about conversation. I learned how to manage my fear and was able to take on greater challenges. I managed to be able to work with people and initiate friendships. Personalities, even disordered ones, can change. Can improve.

Incidentally, a lot of that change came through writing. A large part of Cognitive Behavioural Therapy involves understanding our 'self-talk', the automatic thoughts or commentary that run through our minds, constantly. Because I was shy and depressed, my self-talk about people tended to be very negative. I would automatically think, 'that person thinks I'm stupid. She doesn't want to listen to me. She's looking away, that means she really wants to leave. I'll never be able to talk to anyone. They all think I'm stupid. I'm a hopeless failure'. I would assume all this even before I even spoke to the person.

The therapy for this is to write down those automatic thoughts, that self-talk. I would write it down, then I would write down what I was doing. 'I'm assuming I can read minds', I would write. 'I'm assuming that I know what she's thinking. Moreover, I'm universalising from one situation – I'm assuming that just because this conversation is hard, therefore every conversation will be. I'm catastrophising, making this one conversation mean that my entire life is a failure'.

Then, having recognised what I was doing, I would write down a more rational response. 'I don't know what she is thinking', I would write. 'She might be thinking this is a really interesting conversation. She might have glanced away because that's a natural thing to do. There might have been a sudden flash of light behind me. It doesn't necessarily have anything to do with me. Even if she does want to leave this conversation, that's just one person and one conversation. It doesn't mean it will always happen. My life isn't defined by this one conversation.'

That practice, of writing down thoughts, diagnosing them and challenging them, really works. At the start I had to do it several times a day, for almost every conversation and every situation. With practice, it became more automatic. In time, I could do it on the trot, while the conversation was happening, although even now – after twenty years – I still do it in writing, now and then. Because writing it makes it so much more powerful. It makes me look at my thoughts objectively, and see how wrong they are. How wrong my assumptions about people can be. And it works. This therapy really changed me. I became less anxious, more confident. It truly made a difference.

There are limits, however. I will always be shy and quiet. I will always be introverted, and even if I can now enjoy conversations and people, they will be tiring. Most of all, however much I practice now – however much I have learned skills as a conversationalist – I am not a natural. I'm not very good at talking to people. I'm not very good at just having a conversation.

What, then, about witnessing?

Telling people about Christ is hard. It will almost always challenge and confront people. As our culture moves further away from a concept of absolute truth, the very fact of having a truth that not only disagrees with other people, but that you think others should assent to because it's true – that's quite foreign, and outright objectionable, to most. In a society that, more often than not, moreover, celebrates anti-Christian ethical decisions, Christianity is often considered automatically misguided, if not outright immoral.

It's hard to talk about something that may be considered ridiculous and offensive, untrue and immoral, and may be rudely rejected. It's especially hard to talk about it when it means so much to you. I'm certainly not very good at it.

I have tried a lot. I have tried 'cold call' evangelism, starting conversations around the campus, at bus stops, or knocking on doors. I have spoken to friends and acquaintances, difficult, heart-thumping conversations with desperate mental prayer in the background, afraid of rejection, of being thought arrogant or bigoted or just stupid. I am glad that I have tried; it's always worth trying, always worth giving it a go, always worth trying to get better at doing it. But I do need to acknowledge that God has not really blessed me with that kind of skill. My conversations about God remain, on the whole, awkward and uncomfortable – as far as I can tell, for my listeners as well as for me.

Writing, I can do. Some of my best evangelism has been when I can hand someone a book I have written. Or an article. Or even sending a letter or email. You don't have to think of yourself as a writer – or have anything published – to do the same. Sometimes, writing out what you want to say, what you really want to tell someone from your heart, is the best way of communicating.

Many people struggle with the fear of 'witnessing' – conversations about God. It's odd in one way; God is so central to who we are as believers, and so much a part of our everyday lives, surely He should be as natural a conversation topic as children or spouse or house prices. Yet it doesn't feel like that. This is partly because we live in such a contentious culture, in which personal belief and ethics are particularly contentious. It's partly because it does matter to us so much, and we want to get it right. It's partly because God is no longer a natural topic of conversation; God, and belief, and religion and church and all the associated things, are no longer ordinary topics for newspapers or public discussions or down the pub, in the way that families and house prices are. It's hard to bring God into conversation casually, most of the time. It's hard to think on the spot. It's hard to remember that Bible verse that would be just right for this moment, or to think of the answer to that question. You know there's good reason to think the New Testament is true but you can't remember the details about those manuscripts. You know there's a reply to that argument about the existence of God, but what was it?

Do it in writing. Writing can be done without that adrenaline-fuelled tension. Writing gives you the chance to collect your thoughts and explain what you mean. Imagine objections and questions and give yourself the time to find out the answers. You can put on paper things that just seem too awkward in conversation – 'you seemed surprised the other day when I said I go to church, and I messed up my answer' – 'you mentioned the other day that you don't understand religious people, but there wasn't time just then to explain'. It's sort of like a love letter. It is a love letter, the most love you can ever show someone.

In a letter, too, you can give options for opening the next conversation. Invite your friend to do Bible studies with you, or go to church. Give someone the option of bowing out gracefully, too, in a way that the friendship can still continue.

There are many other ways you can evangelise in writing. Write a blog. Tell your story, why you are a Christian. It's your story, you own it; why not tell it? Write about why you celebrate

Christmas or Easter. Or why you don't. What church means to you. You could write books. You don't even need a publisher these days. Self-Publish on the web. Or on Kindle, or just print a few copies and send them as Christmas or Easter gifts.

I think that writing letters is an opportunity we should make much more of. People love getting handwritten letters. It means that you are really thinking of them, that you care enough to do something concrete. Write letters of condolence or celebration, rather than just relying on a printed card. Letter writing is a much under-appreciated art. You can say so much more, in a more considered way, in a letter; and letters are lovely to receive. They show you have taken the time and effort to consider someone. Don't be afraid to say serious things in a letter. There may be other writers who are more polished, or have a clever turn of phrase, or know more theology than you do. But no one knows your friends or family or immediate social group as you do. No one has that relationship as you do.

Most of all, no one can tell your story as you do. Writing is the chance to explain not just the truths of God, but the difference they have made to you. Say it out loud, tell it in conversation, certainly – but if you can't say it, try writing it. You might find that actually you don't need to send the letter, because having written it and reminded yourself of your love, you now know what to say. You might want to do both.

You may be like me, and never get very good at talking to people. You may be a great talker and find that conversation just comes naturally. Either way, we will all find it hard to tell our friends about Jesus. It's a spiritual battle, and one we need to engage in. But don't think that your methods are all about talking. There are other ways – and often, writing is the best way, a way of being clear, a way of being less directly confrontational. Give it a go, anyway.

ACTIVITY

Write down the ideal conversation you would like to have with your friend about God.

Tell your friend. Or send the letter.

7

Write Bible

It's still Sunday, and I'm in Moore College library, even though the college is still closed to everyone. Late afternoon, so the coffee shops and restaurants are all closed, too. However, I have a college ID card as a Visiting Scholar, and in the college's generosity it is what my brother-in-law calls an Infinity card; it allows me access everywhere, even when there are no staff around. It's wonderful.

Being in the library, I'm enjoying the air conditioning (which is still on, as are the lights) as well as the wi-fi. Did you know wi-fi doesn't mean anything? Or rather, it doesn't stand for anything. It's not a contraction. I just discovered this today. It was a word made up, apparently, by marketers to sound high-tech, a bit like hi-fi which was a contraction of high fidelity. It worked.

The library, and I guess the whole building, is completely empty of people. It's beautifully silent – except for the occasional whine of a mosquito. Goodness knows how they're getting in. I have sprayed myself with insect repellent, liberally, because I seem to have lost any immunity I had to Australian insects. Bites that would once cause only small irritations are now coming up in huge, painful welts. I have one on my forehead that looks like I walked into a door.

My home wi-fi is not working; and one problem with this is that I cannot listen to David Suchet reading the Bible to me every morning. This is a practice I've taken up recently, since I bought Suchet's Bible recording from Audible.[1] He reads to me over breakfast, then I sit and write a Bible meditation before work – by which I mean that I write about the Bible passage I have just heard, things that strike me, things I don't understand, what I think I should do in response. A glorious, wonderful, rewarding space of time – yet sometimes so difficult to bring myself to do it. I am a later riser by nature; left to myself without a timetable, such as right now in the Christmas holiday period, I so easily revert to a pattern of being wide awake until around 2 in the morning, then sleeping until around 10am. At least. It doesn't fit with normal working life, and although in this grant-funded period of time I am blessedly free of most time constraints, I am still aware of the need to use time efficiently. For that reason, I try to fit in with normal work hours. The result is, as with any time that I am working, I am usually late and rushing in the morning.

Taking time to sit and write about the Bible seems, well, a bit indulgent. That's what my instinct keeps telling me in the mornings. I have things to get on with. Stopping to sit down and write in a journal, breaking the flow of the morning, not getting

---

1   It's also available free at BibleGateway.com; or you can buy CDs.

to work – do I really have time? For years, for just this reason, I have done my regular Bible time in the evenings just before sleep. That, and the fact that my brain has not always kicked into gear in the morning. Although, at the end of the day, there is the opposite problem: I need to get to bed, need to get enough sleep for tomorrow. Do I really have the time? Is my brain too sleepy to concentrate? It's going to be a battle, whenever I schedule it.

It was Donald S. Whitney's book, *Spiritual Disciplines for the Christian Life*,[2] that encouraged me to try the mornings. (He has many useful ideas for the spiritual life, including writing). He writes strongly of the importance of Bible meditation, and I found myself agreeing wholeheartedly with him. Spiritual growth comes through being shaped by God's Word; that is the sword of the spirit, the tool the Spirit uses to shape us anew. We need to read and absorb, have the truths of Scripture soak in, creating the framework by which we observe the world, using a few different metaphors. Scripture transforms our minds, gives us categories of understanding and God's way of interpreting our experience.

Such transformation takes time. Most of us would recognise that regular Bible-reading is important. We've probably been told that all our Christian lives; it's the application point of almost any Bible study, any sermon. It's always something we encourage each other to do, always the prayer point that we ask for, that we would read our Bible more. We know it's important, and if you've been a Christian for any length of time, you probably have some system of reading the Bible fairly regularly. That's great.

---

2   Donald S. Whitney, *Spiritual Disciplines for the Christian Life* (Colorado Springs: NavPress, 1991, 2014).

Think, however, of all the other worldview and opinion-forming influences you absorb daily. Social media, what your friends are saying and doing, what the rest of the world is doing, what is trending, the newsworthy items so carefully filtered to shape what you get passionate about. Television, whether news and documentaries or dramas and comedies. Newspapers, in the way they report as well as the opinion pieces. Advertising, which is everywhere. Netflix, Amazon, whatever you watch. Your study or work, your teachers, colleagues and family, Christian and non-Christian. Everywhere there is information shaping your mind, telling you what is good and bad, worthwhile or not worthwhile, important or trivial. Most of it, let's face it, will not reflect God's views on the matter. Most of it won't even acknowledge that He has views.

However, it is God's views that *do* matter. They are the true ones, the authoritative ones. They are the views that will actually reveal to you what reality is; they are the views that are necessary for you to become more spiritual, more godly, more real, more human.

We need Scripture, and we need it deeply. I have tried many different methods of Bible reading; and there are many excellent materials and study notes to help. You can get passages with reflection questions sent to you every day, on your iPad or phone.[3] My problem, however, is that I rush it. I rush through, speed-reading the passage, and then I answer the questions for today's passage in my head. It's too easy to glance at the three or four questions and the paragraphs of notes, think 'yes, great. I know the answer. Done.' I've done my quiet time.

---

3   Try the Explore app, from The Good Book Company; I've found this a
    great way to structure my quiet times daily.

Have I really, though? Often, it has achieved little more than a tick in my mental conscience to-do list. Frankly, I know that if Scripture is going to shape me – if I am going to understand what it actually says in *this* passage other than just repeating to myself truths I already know – I need to try a little harder. Mentally rattling through three questions in a five-minute quiet time won't cut it. I need to slow down, and think a little more.

Writing slows me down. Writing out the answers makes me think harder about them, and makes it much more likely I will remember them. Sometimes I write out the Scripture passage, too. That's another way to emphasise the passage to myself. I might write the whole passage I'm studying, or just a choice quotation. It serves a similar service as underlining or highlighting great verses, or ones that have particularly struck me. Only it's better than just underlining or highlighting. When I take the trouble to write it out, with that hand/mind connection, it makes it stick more. It makes it go deeper.

If I do this in the morning, precisely *because* it feels like I don't have time, it matters more to me. I've been following some of Whitney's suggestions about how to meditate on a passage – rephrasing it in your own words, forming principles from what the text teaches, thinking of analogies or illustrations. Different methods are appropriate for different texts, but they all make you *look* at the text and think about it – and writing it down even more so.

Whitney gives the example of George Muller, the remarkably successful nineteenth-century charitable worker who ran an orphanage in Bristol, England. He was both a deeply spiritual and deeply practical man. 'My practice had been', Muller wrote in 1841, 'at least for ten years previously, as an habitual thing, to give myself to prayer after having dressed in the morning.' He changed that practice, however.

> *Now, I saw that the most important thing was to give myself to the reading of God's Word, and to meditation on it, that thus my heart might be comforted, encouraged, warned, reproved, instructed; and that thus, by means of the Word of God, whilst meditating on it, my heart might be brought into experimental communion with the Lord.*
>
> *I began therefore to meditate on the New Testament from the beginning, early in the morning. The first thing I did, after having asked in a few words of the Lord's blessing upon his precious Word, was to begin to meditate on the Word of God, searching as it were into every verse to get blessing out of it; not for the sake of the public ministry of the Word, not for the sake of preaching on what I had meditated upon, but the sake of obtaining food for my own soul....my inner man almost invariably is even sensibly nourished and strengthened, and that by breakfast time, with rare exceptions, I am in a peaceful if not happy state of heart.*

Muller goes on to speak of how much better his prayer life was once he started doing this. He found that prayer inevitably arose from his meditation on the Bible; it didn't take extra effort, he didn't need separate time for prayer, it just naturally flowed.

Of course it doesn't have to be in the morning. It doesn't have to be by listening, although I recommend David Suchet's marvellous delivery to anyone. Without wi-fi this week, I have returned to reading. Listening, however, like writing, has the advantage that it slows me down. It gives me more time to absorb meaning, and I am less likely to skip over details, especially in very familiar passages which my brain thinks I already know. Someone who is an excellent out-loud reader, as David Suchet is, who has taken the time to study the text him or herself, can add a great deal of comprehension to a passage.

Morning or evening, listening to the Bible or reading it, writing your Bible meditation is an excellent way of making sure you do it properly. I buy myself special Bible-meditation journals which are different from my regular journals. You don't have to; a student notebook from the supermarket works just as well. Keeping to the same notebook or journal is useful because you can see where you're up to, how you're progressing, and you can look over past meditations and so benefit from them again.

Does my suggestion that you take time every day to write a Bible meditation fill you with scepticism? It will take at least half an hour, after all. Fine for you, you might be thinking. But be realistic. I have to get the children breakfasted and ready for school. I have a long commute. I have washing to do, notes to go over. Mornings are too frantic. Evenings are too full.

Did you equally make excuses for other exercises in this book? There is something about Bible meditation, delightful as it sounds, that puts us off far more than, say, writing to reflect on the day, or writing out sorrow or other experiences, or even writing prayer. True, Bible reflection takes mental effort – but I suspect there is a spiritual battle here too. Scripture is the primary means by which you will grow in godliness. It is therefore the one thing that the world, your own sinful nature and the devil will push against and discourage you from doing. I have found, too, that this has been the hardest chapter to write, even though the information in it is not particularly difficult. There is something about considering Scripture that creates a spiritual battle.

Or maybe that's just me.

In any case, the suggestion is still the same. Every morning, every day, write out thoughts on the Bible passage. Use your regular Bible study guide questions, or Bible reading notes; use methods such as summarising, paraphrasing, supplying your own sub-headings, working out applications.

ACTIVITY

Tomorrow, put aside half an hour just to write about a Bible passage. It will be hard to do; you may find you don't have enough to write about to fill a whole half-hour. But try. Set yourself a specific task; for example:

- summarise the passage in your own words
- find one thing you don't understand and write a possible answer
- Write down how you might explain this passage to another person.

If it's hard, try again the next day. And the next. Keep going.

8
The Covid Diaries 2020

When I began this book, I was living a life of unusual freedom, with a six-month grant for writing, with no other duties. I was in a world of coffee shops and conversation, walking down crowded streets and enjoying company. No longer.

I have not had to suffer hospitalisation and the evidently traumatising experience of being on a ventilator in intensive care. I have not had anyone close to me die. I have not been on the frontline caring for the ill. My experience of the time of coronavirus has been relatively comfortable, in a nice flat with access to a garden. I have simply been a person in lockdown by myself, struggling with the normal fears and stress of living in a world during a pandemic. It could be much worse. That has not made it easy.

It's April, and I have been finding it harder, these last few days. More prone to anxiety, harder to get up in the morning, harder to sit down and work, much harder to feel joy. I sit in my window seat and scroll through the day's news, more and more articles about coronavirus that don't mean anything. I sit and almost can't be bothered to click on any particular story, can't be bothered reading to the end when I do. Five ways to care for houseplants during lockdown is about the most intellectual achievement I can manage. Articles about domestic abuse during lockdown break my heart.

I have noticed that the frustration levels are climbing. Outside my house I hear more shouted fights on the footpath, more cars driven at racetrack speeds down our small run of hill. The ground on the corner shows signs of screeching, sliding turns made as fast cars spin out. Many more people out and about, with social distancing only vaguely observed. Lockdown is hard, and there is a limit to how long people will put up with it, it seems. The almost palpable anger in the air transmits itself to me; I don't feel angry, I just feel more wretched.

This morning was especially bad. I planned to go out for a run, but even though the weather was fine – even sunny, between gusts of late April rain – I couldn't get myself out. Too tired, muscles too sore. It probably is okay for me to take a break; I've come back to running after several years, so it's not surprising that the body protests occasionally, and I have been increasing my distances fairly steadily. It's no sin to have a day's rest. However it made me feel a failure, and everything else just made me increasingly grey – the silence of my house, the disinclination to work. My morning prayers failed to break through the grey, even David Suchet's lovely voice didn't do it. Reading the coronavirus news was a big mistake. The USA has over a million cases. No good, no good.

So I roused myself up and went for a walk. Just across the road is a largish wood, on ancient common land, and I have never blessed God so much for it. I have always pictured heaven as an English wood – even long before I had ever seen one. I suppose my ideas were based on Tolkienesque images of Ents and Lothlorien, tales of Robin Hood and probably Brother Cadfael. All no doubt romanticised, and indeed my north-London wood is hardly wild – it is very well looked after by dedicated volunteers – but I have to say it is truly wonderful, and today my ideas of heaven were easy to see. It was wet, but that merely increased its heavy quiet, broken only by gentle birdsong. Paths wander through this wood, surrounded by the intense green of spring growth. It is muddy, but small green leaves are growing up through the mud so that every path has a scattered pattern of greenery. I walked, and thanked God as I walked. For the beauty, for the growing things, for His goodness and purity. I thanked God for all the people I could think of. I thanked Him for His character and greatness.

At one point the path was blocked by overhanging branches drooping heavy with spring blossoms. Tiny white flowers. I stopped and peered close – I wasn't wearing my glasses, one of the everyday things that has gone by the by in lockdown. That might have helped the beauty of the wood, seeing everything in a short-sighted blur, but I don't think it needed much help. I stared at these tiny white blossoms, exquisite and detailed. I was stopped short by their overwhelming loveliness.

Coming home, I felt able to write again, and it is days like this that writing, for me, truly comes into its own. Yes, the walk was a marvellous way to lift my spirits, but I know from experience that that would fade fairly soon once I was inside again, back in the 'real' world. Writing this down, however, has cemented the joyful memory for me. Writing, I am taken back to the dull grey beginning of the day, and why I needed a different perspective

– actually, a more real perspective. Writing it down solidifies in my mind and heart what the right perspective is. I should not focus on the fallen world, which is passing away. Rather, truth is to see the heavenly reality, which is here now, and will last for eternity. Beauty, joy, peace, wonder – these things will last, because they are of God, and as David says, only in Him do we find good. The sorrow, the frustration, the pain of the fallen world – we must do what we can to serve others while we are here, but the way through is to look to Christ and His rescue from the evil of this world. He is the one who will take us to the world in which only the beauty and joy will last, the pain and sorrow will fall away.

I cannot emphasise enough what a difference it makes to write these things down. There is something about writing that connects with the soul. It brings the solace of the lovely walk in the wood in, and I now have confidence that the thankfulness and contemplation of God's goodness which changed me, will continue to do so today. I have bedded it in, and for that I am very thankful.

It has also given me the energy to ring a friend, also in lockdown on her own. I will go and do that now.

A FEW WEEKS LATER.

It turns out that the breathlessness and fatigue I felt on that day, when I could not get myself to run, was actually symptomatic of Covid – yes, I have come down with the virus.

Today, however, for the first time in a few weeks, I woke up this morning clear-headed, energetic, pain-free, positive and smiling. It was astonishing. Not simply in contradistinction to my normal mode of being most definitely a night-owl, not a morning sparrow; but because for the last two weeks I have been suffering from Covid-19, and I most definitely have not woken up that way. My normal waking has been very late in the day, usually with a feeling of exhaustion, severe pain from headaches, with a general malaise of brain fog, aches and pains, and a sense of guilt and failure. Feeling bad in both body and spirit.

Yet today I awoke with joy in the Lord and praise on my heart, literally – my first conscious thoughts were a prayer of praise, of thanksgiving for my life and its struggles which have brought me to where I am now, of praise to the God who is good and great and glorious. I am thankful for everything I have been through, those years of anxiety and depression, the hard work to overcome it, the normal trials of daily life and most recently, this illness; because He has made me into the person I am – still full of faults, true; but so far beyond what I once even thought possible. In me, He has demonstrated the truth of His Word, that suffering brings perseverance, perseverance, character, and character hope.[1] Still a long way to go in the character department, but even glimmerings of hope are enough to transform this existence into joy.

Full of hope, I got up and now I write this down. I knew I must, for even this much clarity of mind will disappear if I do not. I need a record of this moment of perspicuity, in which I am appreciating God, in this small and clouded mind of mine, in some small way for who He truly is. I know my mind; this clarity will soon disappear, I will forget this prayer of praise that sprang spontaneously from my heart, it will be a memory of a good moment without the memory of the true content of that moment. And that's without the effect of Covid, which I doubt I

---

1   Romans 5:3-4.

have suddenly shaken off. Soon, probably within a few hours, I will be full of pain and brain fog again.

So I have written it down, and I am glad. I have a record of God's true grace to me this morning. I can look back at this and know that in this moment, I have apprehended something truly good. Even if I don't read it again, the act of composing these words now and writing them with my hands will have changed my brain, helped tread down and make familiar those occluded neural pathways or whatever metaphor we are using in brain science at the moment. It is not just the moment of praise to God – which is good in itself and if that were all that were possible, it is just as good, and good for me – but I have more, the capacity to make that moment a most solid and enduring and effective part of my life and mental history. Experiencing it was good. Writing it down makes that experience last and become real, so much more. Thank you, Lord.

It is now June, and still I am suffering the ongoing effects of Covid. It just isn't going away: my headaches are getting worse, if anything, agonising spells of pain during which I can only lie down and suffer. The fatigue and brain fog are still there. And today I discovered another downside of Covid – the church I work for has suffered financially during lockdown, and my contract is not going to be renewed. I love this job; I love the people at church, and I have so many plans. Yet it is not to be. And now I am scared, at the prospect that I might not have an income.

But wait. Am I actually going to listen to what I have been teaching others, these many years? Am I going to look to God?

God allows us to go through times of suffering for a number of reasons. It is a punishment for our turning away from Him in rebellion, for eating the fruit, for grasping that right to determine good and evil for ourselves. We could no longer live in a world of paradise in His presence; not just that we no longer deserved it, but that we had corrupted ourselves, reaching beyond our created nature, and so could no longer live forever. What a monstrosity, if the fallen humans we have become were to live forever. We were cast out into a world of death and decay and sin, which means greed and inequality and suffering. We deserve it, and God is merciful that He has not and does not make it much worse.

Occasionally, particular suffering might be in response to a particular sin. That is why it is always appropriate to repent when we are suffering – it might not be a punishment for some particular sin, but we will always have sinned. So it is always right to turn to God in repentance. Can't hurt, anyway. I have been guilty of laziness and taking my pay for granted. I don't know that I am being punished for that, and indeed even if I were, I will not know it until glory. Either way, it is still right for me to be sorry and turn back to God.

God sends suffering to warn us to do just that, too. In the book of Amos, He describes suffering that He sent to His people, and in chapter 4, He describes their wrong response: yet you did not turn back to me. They were meant to turn back. He sent suffering to remind them who He was, as a warning, so that they would turn back. When we suffer, we should take heed and make sure we do so. Any suffering I experience is a reminder to me how much I depend upon Him. I can always turn to Him and always should.

And that is what I have been doing. All this time, I have been determinedly turning to God. I turned initially to God when I was twenty years old, and became a Christian; I think I expected that doing so, suddenly everything in my life would be fixed. It wasn't, of course. Slowly I learned not to blame God for that. Slowly I learned that when the world was not what I wanted it to be, the response is not to cry and rage – even if that crying and raging is in prayer to God. That's better than rejecting Him, but it's still not the right answer.

No, the right answer is to trust Him. To turn towards Him, not away. It's not easy, of course. In fact, it's a miracle of grace when it happens at all. My own willpower can't do it; in fact, in the early years, I didn't even try. Couldn't even try. Even when, as His Word gradually sank into me, I began trying, it was a pathetic effort. It took years of practice, years of effort, years of His Spirit teaching me, for me to start turning to Him more regularly and more completely. This time alone during lockdown, without many of the normal distractions of life, I have been able to turn to Him pretty much daily.

And in doing so, I have been proving true the other reason that God sends suffering – to strengthen us, to strengthen our faith. For God knows that my faith is the most important thing I can have. It is a privilege and a blessing that He wants to strengthen it, that He cares so much for me that He sends me these trials, to strengthen the most valuable thing I have. He wants me to enjoy the blessing of faith; and when I think of it like that, my worry and uncertainty really does fade away. I can trust Him. Whether I end up in a comfortable house with a secure job or not, I can trust him, because He cares so much for me, and proves it over and over.

I want to grow in faith. I want to grow in Christlikeness. How wonderful to be like Christ! To be like Him, in whom all the secrets of wisdom are hid! To be like the perfect human being, the one true human being who perfectly embodies the glory of mankind and the perfect relationship with His father. There is truly nothing better, nothing at all. The joy of knowing myself in Him is the greatest joy possible, and God is offering me that. So I must embrace this uncertainty. I must embrace the loss of these things I have cherished. It is so worth it. My gain from this experience is immeasurable. I am grateful to God for allowing it to happen to me.

We don't seek suffering for its own sake. We are not miserable martyrs, only happy when we're suffering. But we take suffering as the opportunity that it is. It is what makes us like Christ. Its results are overwhelmingly good. I long for security and an end to being alone; I long for a safe place without fear or want or sadness – and I will get it, in the new creation; when Jesus returns, or takes me to meet Him, I will have it. Looking forward to that is another deep comfort in the insecurity of this life. But even right now, with this personal problem of facing joblessness, I can deal with insecurity and discomfort and turn myself away from worry and fear, by knowing what the results of this body blow will be. I will be stronger. My faith will be stronger. I will be ever more able to see God right here, right now. I will be able to live for Him and remain unaffected by the vagaries of the world.

It would be nice to give this book a happy ending, wouldn't it? To end with the news that I found a great job, with lovely people, that I have moved to a beautiful new house somewhere picturesque, with a dog and cats and chickens. Maybe even ducks. That would be a great happy ending.

And yet I think I would like to end this book now, while I still don't know what will happen. While I still suffer attacks of fear, when I wake up with a pang of worry, while I'm still suffering the symptoms of Covid months after I was infected. While I still can't concentrate and don't know when I will be able to again.

While I don't know how I am going to support myself in the coming months. While my headaches are still agony and the painkillers, even the strongest ones that leave me disoriented and entirely unable to think, still don't stop the pain.

I will end here, because it *is* a happy ending. Because nothing has changed. That is, I am in Christ, and nothing can take that away from me. Indeed, the worse things get, the more I am made secure in Christ.

I did not anticipate being here when I began to write. That was a time of great hope and excitement in my life, when I looked forward to a glowing future and was feeling supremely happy about it. Yet here we are, and in God's providence one thing will always be true about the future: we do not know exactly what it will hold. Yet the right response is always the same. Don't be afraid. Trust Him. Whatever it is, He will do what is best for you; most of all, He will teach you to value the things that are actually the valuable things. Security, money, even relationships (which among earthly things are the most valuable) are still perishable things that are only relative in their value. What actually matters is our love of God. That is our real treasure. That, God will multiply and multiply, and we can trust whatever He sends to make it happen.

And – since this book was meant to be about writing – write it all down. So much of my trust in God is actualised and made even stronger by articulating it to myself in this way. It makes a difference, so give it a go. Write godliness. It works.

Appendix : Write As the Puritans Did

The Puritans are much misunderstood, and often ignorantly caricatured. Far from being miserable killjoys, they have written some of the most joyful, uplifting Christian writing in English-speaking history. For those of you who might be interested in the Puritan diary-writing that first caught my eye and inspired the idea for this book, I thought I would share a little of what I found through my historical reading on the subject. I find it fascinating.

As I said in the *Introduction*, I was researching happiness when I happened to come across a paper about the Puritan practice of keeping a diary. This paper described the way in which Puritans would give themselves spiritual counsel in their diaries, to take themselves from sinful frames of mind into a more godly mindset. The paper had come up in my search for information on happiness because evidently such counsel not only brought benefits in godliness, but would also change emotions – the irritability, or despondency, or whatever emotion went along with the sinful actions they tried to change, would actually give way to joy as the diarists exhorted themselves in writing.

What a good idea, I thought. It certainly works for me.

Some Puritan diaries were even written deliberately to be shared with others, to encourage other Christians in similar spiritual self-counsel, and writing such diaries became a fairly common spiritual practice. Well, I thought. Why not do so again?

So I tracked down some of the these Puritan diaries, which give us a model of what they did; but even more useful, I found a Puritan book written about diary-keeping. This was John Beadle's *The Journal or Diary of a Thankful Christian*.[1]

Beadle based his work on Numbers 33:2:

And Moses wrote their goings out, according to their Journeys, by the commandment of the Lord...[2]

This may not be the first verse that springs to mind when you think of journaling! – but Beadle thought this a worthy example to follow. '...they had a Journal of all God's mercies, and why not we a diary of all God's gracious dealings with us?' He is not suggesting that we write scripture, or that Moses' writing is a direct instruction to us, to write; nonetheless, it is a good example for us to follow. If it's good enough for Moses...

But why? What benefit will it be for us to keep a diary? First of all, Beadle encourages us that the worst thing we can do is

1   John Beadle *The Journal or Diary of a Thankful Christian: Presented in some meditations up Numb. 33.2* London, 1656 (London: Forgotten Books, 2017).

2   King James Version.

forget God's goodness. Unfortunately it's also a very common sin.

> *Such is the corruption of all, even the best men by nature, that though in their adversity they seek God early, yet in their prosperity they forget him commonly. They, that in a dark evening are glad of a little star-light, in the day are scarce thankful for the Sun ... It is a most provoking sin to forget God, and the great mercies he hath bestowed on them.*[3]

He reminds us of Luther's warning of the three things that would destroy Christianity: 'carnal security, worldly policy, and forgetfulness of God's benefits.'[4]

That is why, Beadle goes on, God gave His people so many ways of remembering Him: putting fringes on garments, days of feasting, and in the New Testament the Lord's Supper. God also appointed people to write down records so that generations to come would know of His deeds. God wants people to remember what He has done, to continue in thankfulness and to be warned against evil. So, Beadle sums up:

> *To keep a Journall or Diary by us, especially of all God's gracious dealings with us, is a work for a Christian of singular use.*[5]

By this, Beadle meant not just a diary recording places we've been and things that we've done, 'but of the mercies that have been bestowed on us.'[6] In doing so we would be following the example of both David and Moses.

---

3   Beadle, *The Journal or Diary of a Thankful Christian,* pp. 1-2.

4   Ibid., p. 5.

5   Ibid., p. 10.

6   Ibid., p. 11.

So, what does Beadle think we should write about?

Your journal, he writes, should have two types of entries. This first type is about national and public things. Then, you should record personal and private matters. His list of what we should be recording is quite comprehensive, and I must admit I rarely write about 'national and public' matters in my journals; however it's interesting to see the reasons he gives for doing so. He thinks we should 'take notice' of who is leading the country, because rulers influence their people. Also, we should observe what religious principles such people hold, because the best way to govern is based on true religion. These sum up the rest of his recommendations: he wants us to be aware of what is happening in the country, good and bad, and why.

More importantly, Beadle encourages people to see how God is working in our own lives, now and in the past. He encourages us to write about how you became a Christian; how and when it happened, and who was involved. That is the most wonderful thing you can write about:

> it is not only matter of wonder now, but will be cause of admiration unto all eternity.[7]

Note down the times when God is helping you, because we should acknowledge that all we have is from God. Also notice when He helps us withstand temptation and rescues you or others from danger. Give thanks for 'All the instruments, all the men and means that God hath in providence at any time used for our good';[8] such as godly parents, schoolteachers, ministers

---

7   Ibid., p. 51.

8   Ibid., p. 58.

and so on. 'And finally, mark ...what answers God gives to your prayers' because these are 'remarkable pledges of his love'.[9]

In other words, 'Labour by faith to see and observe God in all things that are bestowed on you'[10] – things such as health, peace, liberty, rain, or goods. Be aware of God's fulfilling of His promises, through Christ, and through other people. Observe God's wisdom and goodness in the means He chooses; in His choice of time for answering prayer (and wait for God's time); the fact that He gives enough and not necessarily more.

As you are keeping the diary, Beadle also has advice about how to use it. Read what you have written, often, so you remember how much God has given you, and how much we in our sinfulness need Him. It keeps us humble to be reminded of these things. God does not always give us everything we want; but notice how often He supplies what we need in other ways. You might not have enough of the thing you desire, but what else do you have? Moses, for instance, could not go into Canaan, yet he had an honourable burial. Be reminded of God's providence; and make sure that the lack of one thing does not stop you from recognising all the other good things you have.

While you're at it, remind yourself that the things of this world are not worth running after. Many of the things we desire are empty: we should remind ourselves of the 'vanity of all creature comforts, honours, pleasures, riches, friends'.[11] Don't love them too much, and don't make them idols. Beware covetousness, which not only leads us to lack of gratitude for what we have, but robs us of joy.

---

9   Ibid., p. 62.

10   Ibid., p. 66.

11   Ibid., p. 118.

When you have read your journal, and used it in these ways, Beadle goes on, ask your heart three questions. First, 'What honour do I bring to God for all this?' That is, are you praising God sufficiently and living for Him? Second, 'What good do I to my neighbour?' If God has been generous to you, how are you responding in generosity to others? Finally, 'what good you yourselves get by all that God hath done for you'.[12] In other words, am I making the most of all this health, and wealth and good days? This gospel and this peace? Do I grow?

Make it your work to be thankful for all these things you have reflected on. That is the very point of keeping the journal. Give thanks especially for:

a. Jesus and the unsearchable riches of God's grace in Him
b. Afflictions, which are also God's grace
c. Bless God for every day He has kept you from scandal and sin
d. Bless God not just for what you have, and what you want, but also what you hope to have. There is more to come; we shall enter into joy.

Ask your friends to thank God with you. Don't just ask them to pray for you.

So, Beadle concludes, keep a diary. Too few Christians keep a diary 'of all God's gracious dealings with them'.[13] God wants you to remember what happens in your life, so that you can remember Him. 'It is good therefore not only to remember our low and sinful estate, that we may be humble, but to understand the loving kindness of the Lord, that we may record His favours'.[14]

---

12 Ibid., pp. 112-137.

13 Ibid., p. 152.

14 Ibid., p. 156.

Writing about them is part of studying and understanding them, so make sure you do it.

It is not something that is generally urged as part of Christian duty now, but Beadle certainly thought that keeping a diary – a record of what God is doing in the world, and in your life – is an important part of living as a Christian. He saw this as something almost self-evident. Even heathens keep records, he points out, and this is certainly something that people have done for a long time. We have the example of God himself, who wrote Scripture. So we have every precedent before us, for how important it is to keep a regular record of life. Moreover, it is especially important for Christians to keep a journal, because (Beadle writes with painful truth) your memory is bad and will get worse. To forget God is a sin and the basis of many other sins, and it justly makes God angry.

Keeping a journal will also, Beadle says, help your friends write a history of your life – which probably is not a thought that occurs to most of us, but perhaps suggests that we should make more of an effort to record the lives of faithful brothers and sisters. As well as that, keeping a journal brings 'Christians into great acquaintance with God, and his most gracious nature', so enlarges our love for God, enlarges our hearts in kindness and compassion to our brethren, and will make us humble the more we see God's kindness. Most of all, it will provoke us to thankfulness, and it will help our faith.

All these reasons certainly give us encouragement to keep journals. However, such detailed and daily record-keeping would certainly take time, and a fair bit of effort. Did any Puritans actually take his advice?

The answer is yes, although it is heartening to see that their examples are perhaps more doable than the extremely thorough record-taking described by Beadle. So let us look at one example: the diary of the Puritan preacher, Richard Rogers.[15]

Rogers trained in Christ's College, Cambridge, which was the leading Puritan seminary of the day. He also wrote devotional works which went through many editions. He was writing before Beadle, and he certainly did not follow the first of Beadle's suggestions, to keep detailed records of public events and the times he lived in. However, far more importantly, Rogers' diary could be summarised as being about the struggle to be godly; more particularly, to be in a right frame of mind for godliness.

In another work, Rogers wrote of eight things that the godly Christian should do every day. These included being aware of our sins, being encouraged by God's promise of forgiveness, making sure our hearts are seeking the Lord, reinforcing our own stance against sin, every day nourishing our fear, love and joy of God, thanking Him, praying for steadfastness in doing these things, and going to sleep at peace with God.

These are precisely the sorts of things that Rogers wrote of in his diary. It seems that he strove to keep these habits, not just through prayer and study of the Bible and other books, but also by writing the diary; this would remind him of his resolutions, and give a place to catch himself when straying, and reset himself on the path. He obviously also kept up with Christian companions, and found this very helpful for encouragement in godliness, but keeping a spiritual diary was part of doing the same thing in his personal life.

---

15 Richard Rogers, Samuel Ward, M. M. Knappen, *Two Elizabethan Puritan Diaries* (Delhi, Facsimile Publishers, 2018).

It was also a way of keeping track of his emotions, and bringing emotions back, not just to their proper focus, but to what they should be: real joy and contentment in the gospel, and in gratitude for God's blessings. Rogers, for instance, speaks frequently of emotional pleasure. That's what he's trying to achieve and which he gets from his life. Puritans actually sought, and experienced, great joy. They were never against joyfulness, contrary to the popular picture. They expected, and practiced, that it was entirely right to rejoice in God and his blessings.

This was despite the fact that life was not always easy. Rogers lived through very troubled times. At times he wrote of 'fearful noise of war and trouble in our land', such as attacks from Spain. He suffered loss because of his stand for biblical faith. He experienced the death of his first wife, and of good friends. Yet he always sought a godly response. After one such death, he wrote:

> *And I pray God I may joy less in the world for this cause. I have firmly purposed to make my whole life a meditation of a better life, and godliness in every part, even my occupation and trade, that I may from point to point and from step to step with more watchfulness walk with the Lord. Oh, the infinite gain of it.*[16]

One immediately notable aspect of Rogers' diary is that it was not kept daily – a comfort to those, like me, a little overwhelmed by Beadle's expectations! There are, at times, only one entry per month, summarising what has happened in the past month and reflecting on it: his godly acts, bible study, but mostly how he is in his heart.

---

16   Ibid., p. 64.

At other times entries are more frequent. Usually there is some event in particular that prompts an entry. For instance, Rogers writes:

> *My heart hath been much occupied in thinking of the uncertainty of our life and the momentary brittleness of things below by occasion of the death of Mr Leaper [a local minister]. I find my self at great liberty by this means, when I find a sensible contempt of this world and joyful expectation of departure from hence.*[17]

Other entries take a longer view, seeing his own growth in godliness compared to an earlier time.

> *Thus I have set down some part of those things which have fallen out this month and the sweet peace which I find and feel since I wrote this, which seasons my heart with aptness and willingness to do duty aright, differs unspeakably from that untowardness which before was in me. For in this state my mind is on some good thing with delight and upon transitory things which little regarding them. But before it was my chiefest delight to be thinking upon any profit or vain pleasure, even long before I had to do with them.*[18]

At other times, he is simply depressed by his own ungodliness.

> *August 4, 1587: I cannot yet settle myself to my study [of the Bible], but through unfitness of mind, weakness of body, and partly discontinuing of diligence thereat am held back, and in every kind of it so behind hand, more than some years agone, that I am much discouraged.* [19]

---

17   Ibid., pp. 53-54.

18   Ibid., p. 54.

19   Ibid., p. 56.

I certainly sympathise! I often feel this way myself. Yet this discouragement did not always last, even in the cold of winter:

> *Nov 29, 1587: Since my last writing God continued his kindness to me, for I have had a comfortable and sensible feeling of the contempt of the world and in study, good company, and other peaceable thinking of the liberty and happiness in christianity so occupied that I have not meanly thought of earthly peace or provision, neither of any increasing of our commodities, although god's hand is not shortened to us that way. I thank God... I have not had so continual fitness and cheerfulness of mind to such duties as lay upon me in any manner as here of late.*
>
> *...And this is mine hearty desire that I may make godliness, I mean one part or other of it, to be my delight through my whole life...*
>
> *In my return home my mind by the way was taken up in very heavenly sort, rejoicing not a little that the lord had so enlarged my heart as that my old and accustomed dreams and fantasies of things below were vanished and drowned. The meditations of my heart were such as carried me to the Lord, and full graciously seasoned me against my coming home.*[20]

Rogers often records his feelings going up and down; but it is genuine emotion in godliness. This is understandable: if you have experience of that joy in God and in godliness, which is so hard to obtain because we are sinful, then you know why he goes on about it. Rogers evidently talked to his friends about this, too:

> *After our meeting according to our custom this 30 of November I had a very sweet conference with Mr L. of the practice of godliness, of the necessary fruit and comfort of it, of the way to bring it forth.*

---

20   Ibid., p. 65-67.

> *After, at night, we had a meeting, a bethinking of ourselves how we might rouse up ourselves to a father care of beseeming the gospel, which was very fruitful. After this also I was in comfortable plight, feeling no hindrance from having my heart upon the Lord.[21]*

Rogers' emotions were very important to him, not just because he wanted what Scripture commanded – joy in God – but also because it was such a strong motivator for him to godly action. And a good way to get himself into this more godly frame of mind, which was not just more enjoyable, but would spur him on to further godliness, he wrote about it.

> *July 9 1589: Reading the writings of another brother about his estate an hour and longer, I was moved to write, and to bring my heart into a better frame, which in the beginning was impossible to me, but, I thank God, I feel a sensible change of that, and will set down after how my heart grows better seasoned.[22]*

One excellent example is his encouragement to himself when he was suspended from ministry because of his Puritan principles.

> *Nov 3 1589: It is one of the greatest crosses which could have befallen me, so I saw it very necessary to stay up my weakness with some strength of persuasions to rest contented and thankful to God under it, and prepared with fit readiness and cheerfulness to any good which my place may yield. As first this was one:*
>
> *1. Seeing it is of the Lord, his will, and thus good reason it should be mine.*
>
> *2. Seeing I have enjoyed comfortable liberty so long.*

---

21 Ibid., p. 68-69.

22 Ibid., p. 84.

3. *Seeing I did not honour God in studying for my sermons as sometime, and as I should have done.*

4. *Seeing it is the lot of my betters, yea and a heavier portion than this also, as deprivation of living, imprisonment.*

5. *Seeing my beginning how unlike I was, not only not to govern myself, but much less a part of God's church. I have no cause to take it hardly.*

6. *Seeing the iniquity of the time affords no better thing, but grows to hinder and cut down those means which are seen to stop the cause of sin most.*

7. *Seeing God, by this, means to rouse me from making this world my heaven, which, as I am like enough to offend in and go maying in respect of my corruption, so the rather for that many good men are deceived with it.*

8. *Seeing the Lord will exercise my faith, patience, obedience etc hereby.*

9. *Seeing he will prepare me for greater afflictions by this.*

10. *Seeing he would keep me from further corruption of the time, which might, by little and little, winning ground in me, blindfold my judgement and weaken that little measure of good conscience, godly zeal, and courage for the glory of God, which is in me, wherein I pray God that our coldness, in giving place to all that is thrust upon us, be not laid to our charge, while none stand up against it.*

11. *Seeing the Lord leaves many encouragements to me, in respect of many other, both in the people's love, and in communion with them, and otherwise.*

12. *Seeing I suffer not, though the reproach and grief and discommodity be great, not as an evil doer, but for the quietness of my conscience, 1 Peter 3.[23]*

---

23 Ibid., p. 91.

How might this translate to a modern journal entry? I'm in a slightly different situation, so I would change some things, but this is what I could have written after receiving the phone call telling me that my job was ending.

Losing my income, and my house, is one of the most frightening things I have ever faced, so to help me in my weakness, I will try to persuade myself to be contented and even thankful to God for this news, and prepare to accept cheerfully whatever good may come of it.

1. *This decision is God's will, and that's good enough reason for it to be my will as well.*

2. *I have enjoyed this job, and my lovely flat, for nearly 12 months now; that's a blessing.*

3. *It's not as if I deserve anything, after all. I haven't always worked hard, I could have served people better. I have had times of laziness.*

4. *People have suffered much worse than I have.*

5. *I have been saved from death to life. God has been so good to me.*

6. *Times are tough for lots of people.*

7. *God can use this situation to stop me from depending upon worldly things too much, or thinking that this world is where I should look to fulfil my desires. I might have even been teaching others to think the same.*

8. *God will strengthen my faith, patience and obedience through this.*

9. *He will also prepare me for even worse suffering, if that should happen.*

10. *He is keeping me from further worldliness, which I'm only too tempted to.*

11. *There are so many other good things that I have. I have loving Christian friends, and family, and I will not be left destitute. (This really was something that I used to encourage myself.)*

God truly is good. As the Puritans knew, we are all too ready to forget His goodness, and to magnify bad things as if they are what really matters. Going through a reasoning process such as the above is so helpful, and means that what God is teaching us becomes much more our focus. A truly spiritual journal is not just me expressing my sad feelings – therapeutic though that can be – but going through a process to turn around my feelings, and thoughts, so I can genuinely see the good that is happening. It is always there. We can trust Him.

Acknowledgements

Thanks to all the people who made my study break in Australia so enjoyable. Thanks also to Christian Focus, for their help, encouragement, and lovely cover art. Anne Norrie, my editor, did an excellent job. Everything else is my fault.

Most of this book was handwritten with a Lamy fountain pen in a Paperblanks journal.

Christian Focus Publications

Our mission statement –

STAYING FAITHFUL

In dependence upon God we seek to impact the world through literature faithful to His infallible Word, the Bible. Our aim is to ensure that the Lord Jesus Christ is presented as the only hope to obtain forgiveness of sin, live a useful life and look forward to heaven with Him.

Our Books are published in four imprints:

CHRISTIAN
FOCUS

popular works including biographies, commentaries, basic doctrine and Christian living.

CHRISTIAN
HERITAGE

books representing some of the best material from the rich heritage of the church.

MENTOR

books written at a level suitable for Bible College and seminary students, pastors, and other serious readers. The imprint includes commentaries, doctrinal studies, examination of current issues and church history.

CF4•K

children's books for quality Bible teaching and for all age groups: Sunday school curriculum, puzzle and activity books; personal and family devotional titles, biographies and inspirational stories – Because you are never too young to know Jesus!

Christian Focus Publications Ltd,
Geanies House, Fearn, Ross-shire,
IV20 1TW, Scotland, United Kingdom.
www.christianfocus.com